Global Citizenship *and* Social Movements

Global Citizenship *and* Social Movements

Creating Transcultural Webs of Meaning for the New Millennium

Janet J. McIntyre-Mills

Routledge
Taylor & Francis Group
LONDON AND NEW YORK

Published by Routledge
2 Park Square, Milton Park, Abingdon, Oxon, OX14 4RN
270 Madison Ave, New York NY 10016

Transferred to Digital Printing 2008

British Library Cataloguing in Publishing Data

McIntyre-Mills, Janet J.
Global citizenship and social movements : creating transcultural webs of meaning for the new millennium
1.Knowledge, Sociology of 2.Communication – International cooperation – Social aspects 3.Intercultural communication 4.Social change 5.Sustainable development – Social aspects
I.Title
303.4'82

ISBN 90-5702-590-6

Publisher's Note
The publisher has gone to great lengths to ensure the quality of this reprint but points out that some imperfections in the original may be apparent.

This book is dedicated to *Adelaide Dlamini* of Guguletu, Cape Town, an indigenous healer who taught me the meaning of integrated, inclusive thinking, and to my graduate students, particularly *Denys Delaney*, with whom some of these ideas have been developed.

Contents

Acknowledgments

I am particularly grateful for the comments by Dr. Norma Romm and Professor Adam Jamrozik on sections of this work; however, any shortcomings are mine alone.

1

Introduction

This essay is based on my varied experiences as a researcher and as a university and community educator, facilitator and planner in a wide range of contexts. The focus of my development work—theoretical, practical and applied—has been to understand the way in which social problems are constructed by different interest groups. So much energy is focused on solving problems without agreement on the nature of the problem. The way reality is constructed is based on our assumptions and values. The first goal of this essay is to convince the reader that inclusive thinking, which traces common webs of meaning across the separate frameworks of cultural and social values, can be taught by means of thinking tools. People can be educated to work with ideas and assumptions rather than within the boundaries of a prescribed orthodoxy. The second goal is to argue that tools for thinking and communicating can help us re-work the categories that limit our thinking by forging transcultural webs of meaning.

Webs are created as a result of a belief that by virtue of our common humanity and common environment, we need to co-create our futures. Mapping the different perceptions of interest groups and ascertaining the reasons why people think in particular ways are the first steps for working together. By using a range of thinking tools, we can help interest groups think beyond frameworks of meaning and, instead, think in terms of links, overlaps and webs. This could enhance the likelihood that people will choose "pooling, allying and linking" (to use Moss-Kanter's, 1989 term in a broader sense) to solve problems. Such an approach makes more sense in terms of our long-term survival as human beings on this planet. By using group work skills together with problem-solving techniques, common ground can be created, provided the socio-political and economic contexts in which we work are clearly understood and the political will to cooperate exists or is created as a result of a realization that we share one environment and similar needs because, biologically, we are "of one body". The processes involved encompass more than merely sharing information and building alliances. They also involve helping interest groups to abandon the notion of closed frameworks for understanding.

Recent experience of working in the arid zone of Central Australia, Alice Springs highlights the need to find sustainable development solutions. Alice Springs is a borderlands of cultures. The First Australians are concentrated in this urban centre and the cultural diversity is heightened by large numbers of international and local travellers and immigrants from European and Asian countries. The First Australians, no longer restricted by government wardships or missions, have resumed moving across the land as they did prior to colonisation. This movement between urban areas and 'country', along with land title, must also be considered as an indigenous ***social movement*** and a challenge to their status as the most marginalised of all Australians (Coulehan, 1998).

The effects of colonisation on Aboriginal people are still visible in terms of all social health indicators, for instance: the highest incarceration rates 'courtesy' of a Northern Territory law called mandatory sentencing, unemployment rates, morbidity and mortality rates. Poor diet, extensive use of alcohol and risk-taking behaviour are associated with a sense of having little personal control over their lives. This leads to high injury rates.[1] The notion of being a nation within a nation is, however, a powerful reply to this sense of being treated as second-class citizens. Their sense of national identity is built upon a sense of the sustainability of the environment, through living in harmony within a fragile arid zone. The liberative potential of this concept of nationality lies in the potential to contribute to the social movement for an ecologically sustainable future.

The lack of effective communication across cultures underlines the need for transcultural thinking tools that can facilitate mutual understanding and assist in developing a shared political will based on a belief that all cultural maps have creative potential. By learning to consider the way in which cultural maps can overlap, extend and complement one another, problem-solving can be made easier. Ecological and humanistic thinking are required for solving some of the toughest challenges in the next millennium.

The world we live in today has two opposing dynamics: globalisation of the economy and an approach to social change based on a sense of shared interests, which lead to wide-ranging social movements. Biologically, human beings have in common one environment and shared human needs. Political and economic common denominators are increasingly recognised. Simultaneously, a strong tendency exists to splinter off from a shared sense of global interests, to fragment into nation states and for political parties to step back in time to a bounded set of ethnocentric and/or nationalistic policies. These paradoxical characteristics need to be addressed.

Without cooperation and the recognition of common goals we are doomed to conflict and the waste of human and natural resources, therefore competition is harmful and irrational, rather than rational economic behaviour.

It is assumed throughout that:

- responsible global citizenship is a process and goal of development;
- the nature of social development can only be defined in terms of intersubjective dialogue;
- the closest we can get to 'truth' is through trying to see the point of view of all the stakeholders within specific sociocultural, political and economic contexts.

A nihilistic notion of extreme relativism is avoided because if there are no absolutes there can be no recognition of the imperative to recognise our sharedness, which is vital for social justice and survival of systems. Recognition of the balance between diversity and common denominators is the goal of global rights and responsibility. It is based on the normative assumption that by virtue of our common humanity, we do have common denominators: similar biology and one ecosystem to meet our shared needs:

—Private troubles and public issues are central concerns of a social justice that is sensitive to differences in life chances.

—Critical thinking tools can be developed for creative thinking and problem-solving across disciplinary boundaries. The interlinked world of private enterprise and the contracting public welfare sector need to be explored.

—Social change is only possible by expanding the power base of concerned interest groups. Social movements are the political vehicles of concerned interest groups. Only wide-ranging networks set up by a host of social movements concerned about "staying" the so-called hidden hand of the rational market can provide an equal balance. Stretton's (1990) unpublished paper, "Australia on the road to Mexico," argues that "Most of the serious difficulties in resuming sovereignty over our economy are not technical, but political" (p45). The essence of his argument is that political parties to the Right and Left in Australia have from the time of Paul Keating, allowed the markets to dictate. In his opinion strong opposition is required to restore faith in limited control of markets. The re-introduction of a version of Keynesianism seems to be the thrust of his paper. He advocates a strong trade union movement to challenge current policies. But adopting a much broader social movement approach could increase the likelihood of change.

—We need creative thinking tools for the new millennium to address the fallout caused by rapacious forms of capitalism and socialism. Economic rationalism is a current orthodoxy, which appeared to be self-producing only because the model has been reified into an artificially closed system. Once its flaws became apparent as a result of the collapse of economies, even the most mainstream economists have begun to question the unrestrained rule of markets. The need to intervene and not allow markets to dictate has become a policy agenda once again. What is needed is much greater re-consideration of the nature of economics, the environment and sustainable social justice. This requires setting aside the sort of technocratic thinking that involves concentrating on the visible, the concrete without unpacking the reason why a social issue or disease occurs. The clinical response is a prescription. The economic rationalist response is to continue to apply 'the market rules' philosophy. The social work response is to ameliorate with welfare programs and projects without rethinking structure. Technocratic thinking, if used alone, has a "go no further effect" (Zola, 1975). Technocratic thinking is not to be confused with the creative application of technology together with a critical approach to solving problems. Technology, *per se,* is not the problem. It is only a problem when technology is seen as an end in itself without considering wider issues.

Culture is the set of learned ideas and behaviour that groups of people develop in relation to their environment. Culture is a way of life; it is the way people express themselves in social, political and economic terms in response to their natural environment. Culture includes ideas and values about the social, the built and cultivated, and the natural environments.

Although separate cultures need to be given some unfettered individual space to preserve diversity, the common needs of the environment should be held uppermost. Human beings as global citizens must remember their individual rights and collective responsibilities. This work highlights a belief in the ability of human beings to map their world rationally in reaction to strands of postmodernism, which cynically set aside the notion that any absolutes exist.

The roots of cultural mapping lie in many disciplines. Historians, travel writers, early ethnographers, sociologists and social anthropologists mapped the picture of culture from the point of view of the early settlers. The colonial and masculine viewpoints have been challenged and expanded by feminist "herstories" and indigenous stories, which tell of the same events from different sets of assumptions and values. Mythology, history and "herstory" have equal status in cultural maps. Cultural mapping can represent multiple points of view. As such, it can be a vehicle for achieving mutual understanding and respect for cultural diversity. The goal of cultural mapping is an appreciation that the overlays of many perspectives enrich and expand human understanding. A key function of cultural mapping is to identify information for problem-solving to ensure that human and natural resources are used to the benefit of all citizens. The challenge is to integrate ideas without sacrificing the representation of diversity. This can be achieved by ensuring that each theme is mapped using multiple overlays of paradigms. Cultural maps need to be linked and overlaid so as to benefit from seeing one social issue from many perspectives.

The process for celebrating diversity and preserving creative rights whilst developing collective responsibility is paradigm dialogue (PD). This volume develops a definition of PD and its implications for systemic thinking. Participation as a panel member in a session entitled 'Paradigm Dialogue' (PD) at the 14th World Congress of Sociology in Montreal served to underline and develop the specific way in which the concept is used in this argument. In everyday life, PD is about the mechanics and ethics of having a democratic conversation that enables all participants to express their points of view and be listened to with respect. The assumptions are humanistic (Smaling, 1998). PD ensures that researchers using particular research methodologies engage in dialogue with those using different methodologies to prevent misunderstanding a slice of reality (Blaikie, 1998, Romm, 1998). More specifically, PD can be used to bring about democratic changes in a range of applied-action research contexts. The implications for praxis are important (Weil, 1998). The version outlined below includes all these definitions of PD but argues that PD is also about reconsidering: a) the nature of knowledge; b) the process of creating knowing and c) the implications of adopting open and closed stances to paradigms for our human and ecological future. This work attempts to address interlinked socio, cultural and ecological concerns locally and globally. The approach is transdisciplinary and explores concepts not normally considered in juxtaposition. The argument is wide-ranging and spans disciplinary parameters, it emphasises the need for theoretical and methodological literacy in order to address complex social problems.

PD extracts the liberative potential from paradigms rather than pitting one paradigm against another in a competitive way. The argument developed below cannot be dismissed by some as "warm fuzzy thinking", because our welfare and that of our ecosystem depends on the ability of human rationality to evolve from thinking in categories to thinking systemically. The goal of PD is to use thinking tools to extract the 'liberative potential' (Gouldner, 1971, 1980) from a wide range of ideas in order to solve complex social and environmental concerns.

Human beings are not the same as animals. We are not programmed entirely by instinct; we are able to be reflexive about our thinking even though we may be limited by the extent of our knowledge, which is contextual. Aristotelian logic organises and controls by classifying phenomena. Discourses embody binary oppositions: yes/no, black/white, self/other, right/wrong, civilised/uncivilised, normal/abnormal, pure/impure, safe/dangerous. Foucault (1967) explores the space or divide between self and "other" created by thinking spatially in terms of categories. Knowledge is based on antagonism, competition and "fighting for territory" and defending it through drawing the "line in the sand" and through alienation. Foucault meticulously examines the implications of binary oppositions in human knowledge and human organisation.

The enlightenment version of humanist thinking based on the essential rationality of human beings led to control and power over others and nature. 'Power over' requires maintaining the separation between "Self" and "Other". Human beings were deemed able to "tame", "civilise" and "colonise" nature and "the other". Despite this, it is undeniable that Aristotle's approach to dialogue did have potential. Unlike Plato, however, instead of engaging in dialogue to find knowledge through unity and seeing the bigger picture, he developed the notion of divisions in order to make sense of the world. Thus it did not follow through the dialectical potential of his version of dialogue that silenced the opposition once it had engaged in a win-lose dialogue. This became the imperative of science.

> What needs to be underlined here is that the successful and largely unchallenged establishment of an empirical mode of thought led away from any temptation to indulge in the construction of an intellectual or theoretical totality. If the world is composed of millions of empirical situations, it can be catalogued, but not captured in a single *a priori* theory or overriding explanation, with the crucial exception of the mind of God. In this perspective, theories are just the accumulative and organisational frameworks of so many facts that make up an ultimately knowable world. It involves an implicit and unacknowledged metaphysics of its own—the stable referent of an irrefutable and independently verifiable world—that was usually displaced into the apparently neutral language of 'science' and 'learning' (Chambers, 1990).

It is argued that the closest we can get to truth is through dialogue. But, paradoxically, a celebration of diversity cannot silence the one ultimate truth: namely, that human beings are systemically linked to one another and to their ecosystem. This essay explores and celebrates the human paradox—the will to be a creative individual and active agent and the necessity to be part of a collective system.

This acknowledgement of our interlinked reality does not mean that the rich and powerful should have the right to pit nature against the rights of people, particularly those who are less economically dominant in terms of current standards. Ecological thinking is about solving problems through understanding systemically rather than apportioning blame to 'the other'.

Colinvaux (1978, 1980) argues that species of animals and the species Homo Sapiens compete for scarce resources. Human beings try to maximise their survival by maximising the number of their offspring through developing a cultural niche, which initially was geographically limited. But as creative people developed technology and as trade developed, some were able to claim wider niches. These gave them power over others of the same species. All people share, biologically, a common genotype, with very superficial physical differences, but are able to use culture ingeniously to adapt to different environments. Human beings form one species and have in common one environment. Thus, national identities have been used as a means of differentiating one group from another and as a means of competing for scarce resources.

If we take the ecological thesis seriously, as human beings develop technology and expand their niche to serve the interests of their children at the expense of those of other nations, we could lapse into a type of fatalistic cynicism borne of the belief that human beings are programmed by instinct in the same way that animals are programmed. The notion of forging webs of common global understanding and knowledge would be impossible if this were the case. Another debilitating thought process is the postmodern idea that there is no ultimate truth or reality for which to strive and no such thing as a shared rational goal or common denominator by virtue of our common humanity and environment. This would allow human beings to lapse into nihilism and fatalism.

No matter how we construct our lives as individuals, and no matter how we choose to celebrate our diversity by means of separate identities, we cannot as rational beings deny the reality of our sharedness—in terms of biology and ecology—if we wish to survive. Cultural diversity is a result of the interaction of people living in different parts of the ecosystem and adapting to their environments. This lived experience is the heritage of years of cultural learning by trial and error.

Nations as categories emphasise categorical differences that have led to competition between groups. The ability to survive in the long term is based on our potential ability to think collectively rather than competitively in terms of environmental, national, or class spaces. In this respect, the Hobbesian notion that "nature is red in tooth and claw" is only half true; human competitive instincts have been successfully shaped through philosophical development to appreciate the benefits of democracy, even if democracies in their current forms only achieve partial justice. This shift in thinking does not require altruism, merely a rational mind that recognises the advantages of mutual survival as opposed to mutual annihilation based on 'us' versus 'them'. Possession of superior technology according to Colinvaux (1980) in *The Fates of Nations* has throughout history led to the ability to conquer others and thus to ensure the survival of the group at the expense of 'the other'. Technological development has progressed to the level where we have developed a 'risk society' (Beck, 1992) in which there can be no winners in a wasteland.

Technology can, however, be used creatively for the development of transcultural webs of understanding for the mutual benefit of people and the environment. Computer technology and social movements can make this possible if we assume that we have more to gain by cooperating. This argument is developed in chapters 4–6.

A Critical and Ecological Humanism strives, through the vehicle of paradigm dialogue, to remove the 'false consciousness' rooted in the heritage of binary oppositional logic. This work explores the liberative potential of Hegelian dialectics, in order to rediscover the wisdom of holistic thinking without denying the pervasive existence of binary oppositional discourses that can be argued to be a source of social, political and economic adversity. If we see the links across phenomena instead of organising phenomena in boxed categories, we are able to think in terms of affiliation rather than competition. The ontological assumptions of this work are both humanistic and ecosystemic. The vehicle for creating and recognising links is paradigm dialogue, in order to create a language that recognises both common denominators and diversity.

Thinking tools help to shift thinking away from simplistic structures and models to thinking that traces contours across paradigms. Whereas categories alienate and are divisive, webs affiliate and create a sense of shared meaning. Paradigm dialogue is liberative and can heal rifts by closing the spaces through recognition of the links that bind people together in one ecosystem. This is a revised version of humanism, one that places people *within* ecosystems rather than *above* ecosystems. An Ecological and Critical Humanism (EcoHumanism) is a rational, ethical and political response to the real dangers facing human beings within their ecosystem. Critical is used in the sense of reflexive, dialectical, creative and exploratory.

Compassion for the 'other' cannot be taught as a competency, but we can be made aware through reflexive thinking that the closest we can ever get to a shared truth and sustainable social justice is through listening to and striving to understand the other. By virtue of our shared humanity and environment, we are systemically linked. We need to understand that by seeing the links across social and environmental phenomena, we can begin to move away from the sort of thinking that splits and separates phenomena into categories (Flood, 1998:96). Logically, however, if we think in adversarial terms, then tools for destruction make sense until we realise that we can never create a boundary between ourselves and 'the other' as winners and losers because we are bound together in one ecosystem.

Ultimately, systems are only as strong as their weakest sections; we are indeed linked. The effects of exploitation, pollution and poverty cannot be quarantined, as Beck (1992) has emphasised in *Risk Society*. The technology to create life (human, animal and plant), to create artificial worlds, to travel through space and potentially colonise other systems, and the technology to destroy our own ecosystem are no longer science fiction but an awful reality. We can co-create or destroy at our own risk.

There is a realisation amongst some thinkers that the environment as a whole is a limited resource and that the best way to conserve it and our own place in it is through cooperation with one another. Ulrich Beck, for instance, has stressed that the "boomerang" effect of pollution will eventually affect the rich and the poor, because pollution has no boundaries and eventually no amount of money will be adequate to buy a safe environment. A warning has been sounded, however, by Castells (1996). Technological "haves" (nations and classes) are part of the networked society by virtue of information technology and are therefore part of the global economy. Those who are marginalised through lack of access to information, power and capital could be consigned to unprotected and polluted suburbs, outer cities or regions. This is a hypothetical scenario, but one which has become increasingly possible if the divide between the technological "haves" and "have nots" continues to grow.

How can the big questions be addressed if around dinner tables in the most "civilised" of suburbs in the most "civilised of nations" the bases of discrimination are thinly veiled? Discrimination against some category of people on the basis of some criterion of difference illustrates the notion of thinking in terms of categories of 'self" versus 'other'. If global citizenship is redefined as a sense of global rights and responsibilities, a sense of interconnectedness and a respect for the value of diversity needs to be cultivated. This requires 'both and' thinking rather than 'either or' thinking. It requires a shift away from thinking in terms of frames or paradigmatic boxes and categories and a shift towards thinking in terms of webs. Individual rights can only be maintained through allowing for diversity and this in turn is vital for creative thinking. As Weber (see *Economy and Society*, 1978) has stressed, the efficiency of bureaucracy has the downside of stifling creativity in the bid to control and standardise organisational activity. The only limit on

individual creativity should be a responsible concern for the rights of 'the other' and for the environment.

At this point, intellectual and reproductive creativity need to be considered. Colinvaux (1986) makes the biological observation that as technology has provided more resources, so the population has increased beyond the level at which everyone can live a dignified life based on freedom, equality and fraternity. He denies that it would be possible to change demographic transitions successfully by merely ensuring the improvement in the quality of life of the poorest of the poor to the level of the richest. He argues instead for a shift in cultural thinking so as to use technology in harmony with nature for sustainable development options. He emphasises that premodern cultures should be studied, as they provide successful models. Others such as Nobuko (1998) have argued convincingly for the need to shift from development to the enhancement of sustainable life-styles.

Strehlow (1978:24–25), whilst studying the Arranda in the 1940s, emphasised that Australian Aboriginal people had been gravely misunderstood:

> The crude and by now, it is hoped, completely exploded view that the Aboriginal Australians had remained at such a low level in their mental evolution that they had no knowledge whatever of physiological paternity, and that they were incapable of seeing the difference between themselves and the animals (or plants or natural phenomena) that constituted their totems, has no foundation in fact. When an Aranda man declared to a white questioner that he was a honey-ant, a kangaroo, an emu, and so on, he was merely using normal abridged formula for stating his totem, relying—as he could among his own tribesmen—on the common-sense of his white interrogator to interpret his answer. It did not occur to him than any white man could be so stupid as to regard him as a moron incapable of knowing the difference between men and animals . . . . .

Strehlow, like many who have attempted to understand the 'other' from the position of 'expert', did not, however, live up to his own ideals in practice. According to Gradey (in Bowden, 1994:17), as Protector he discouraged respect by supporting changes to religious ceremonies and disregarded the wishes of Aboriginal elders by removing religious artifacts, for example. The Strehlow Centre is also explicitly criticised in the Central Land Commission's Annual Review (1997/1998:37) for not returning artefacts to the original owners.

To what extent can 'the other' ever be understood in an unmediated way? So-called advanced nations and classes assume that they have all the answers, based on their privileged consumption of educational and information resources. My response is in the form of another question; namely: what are the implications of not understanding the other? The imposition of solutions, which are in the interests of the most powerful groups, is one possibility. The impact on life chances for the less powerful, and for parts of the planet used for dumping and extraction, could be the outcome. It is undeniable that in some instances a sufficient number of common denominators will not be recognised by groups. When opposition cannot be resolved, then a decision has to be taken to disagree until shifts in thinking can occur as a result of dialogue facilitated through educational social movements in a range of domains. The potential for violence has heightened because nuclear disarmament has been agreed to by some nations but not by all, and the proliferation of nuclear nations underlines that the danger remains very real as we face the new millennium. The notion that violence is acceptable as a last resort is no longer a viable option because there can be no winners. Bearing this in mind, it can be argued that problem-solving through dialogue is the only way to achieve global citizenship.

A realisation that perhaps there is more than one way of seeing leads to an understanding that when doing problem-solv-

ing at any level, local, national or international, there may be more than one answer. The privileging of more than one voice is only possible when dialogue is maintained so that we can learn from one another. The assumption that truth is dialogue leads to a realisation that if global knowledge is to be a goal of research and problem-solving, then the tension between local diversity and common denominators based on common humanity is our goal. What we mean by our common humanity needs to be co-created through dialogue. The political will for negotiation is reasonably survival. According to Romm (1997, personal communication), "what our common humanity is, itself has to be continuously negotiated. There is no 'sharedness' independently of finding 'common' meeting points". Defining what these may mean also moves away from simplistic "modernist, enlightenment" readings of "common humanity". It recognises the tensions involved in discussing our 'sharedness.'

Singer (1993) points out the need to see the connections amongst apparently innocent choices made by the rich—such as to eat red meat regularly, or to use chemicals for household cleaning, or to drive to work everyday, to mention just a few—and the implications they have on the sustainability of the environment. Collaboration, not competition, is the hallmark of the new era of global citizenship and human rights and responsibility. Being able to think holistically and 'remaking the connections' (Smith and Williams, 1992) amongst humans, animals and their environment is the new rational imperative, which can be politically addressed only through social movements geared at engaging in dialogue across paradigms, as discussed in more detail later.

Reconceptualising Citizenship for 200 and Beyond

This we know, the earth does not belong to man, man belongs to the earth. This we know, all things are connected, like the blood

which unites one family. All things are connected. Whatever befalls the earth, befalls the sons of earth. Man did not weave the web of life. He is merely a strand in it. Whatever he does to the web, he does to himself (Chief Seattle, quoted in Doel and Shardlow, 1996).

When you watch a spider build its web, the whole structure interacts and binds the web together with diagonal, horizontal and vertical ties to give it strength and stability. . . .We must continue to be like the spider's web. . .linked to each other. . .giving strength to each other. . .(Geoff Shaw, 1998).[2]

The commonly held definition of global citizenship means (to some): 1) the freedom to travel to economies with weak currencies; 2) to profit from the open markets; 3) to use hedge funds to de-value weak currencies; 4) that it gives the freedom to the educated and wealthy to create international careers or business opportunities; 5) the power of rich nations and classes to blame poor nations and classes for environmental problems and 6) the terrifying notion of one global state with ultimate power.

The totalitarian state is not the flip-side of the concept of global citizenship that I propose. The arrogant attitude expressed by professionals and business people who feel "at home in any major city" because "whether they are in Manila, Sydney or Los Angeles, a luxury hotel, corporate headquarters or private hospital are not very different" does not encapsulate the sense of global citizenship used in this work. Nor is that sense expressed by the committed corporate businessperson whose standard office environment reflects local culture merely by means of token items of local art and artefacts, without an in-depth reflection on the similarities, overlaps and divergences in cultural maps.

Those trapped by limitations are "acted upon" rather than powerful actors. A revised definition of citizenship is concerned about the way in which the resource and information poor can compete with empowered mobile capital without resorting to nationalism or fundamentalism (Castells 1997). This notion of global citizenship challenges, extends and revises Marshall's (1977) original notion of social rights and responsibilities, and explicitly emphasises not only the public sphere but the private and community sphere. There, many marginalised people, particularly women, have operated, without much recognition, in order to work collectively for the good of their families (Weeks, 1996). Definitions of citizenship have previously considered the rights and responsibilities (social, political and economic) within the national context. The right, for example, to free speech, free media, the right to vote, to own land, to employment, to a fair trial continue to be a long way off for many people at a national level as a result of government decisions.

Democratic rights are merely a dream for many people who are not citizens in any sense of the word. Even within so-called democracies, the shifts away from universal to residual welfare limit the rights of the unemployed, who are now less likely to be entitled to a social wage. Citizens who do not work or are physically or mentally unable to work are socially stigmatised in many ways (Pixley, 1993, Tomlinson, 1996); and it is vital to note that in democratic states the rights to land continue to be debated in the form of First Nations versus Colonisers. For example, the Sioux, Inuit, and Aboriginal Australians emphasise that they are the caretakers of the land for their children and that their health is linked to the health of the land. Ecological humanism needs to be the goal of all citizens, not only those who regard themselves as "first nations". As Castells (1997) stressed, national identity, citizenship and the state do not always overlap. Nationality may be used to undermine or build states and some national identities may be recognised as citizens and others not. The goal of global citizenship is to forge a new identity as a species (Castells, 1997:127). The aim of this essay is to discuss the ways in which we can discard nationalism; categorical and competitive thinking that strives to fight for territory by means of win-lose, and binary oppositional thinking.

The concept of global citizenship shifts rights and responsibilities from a national to an international context. It revises social goals that are blueprinted to social goals which are constantly redefined through dialogue to **establish contracts** by making use of computer, video, and phone technology for regular input from the full spectrum of citizens. This includes the technologically poor through specifically providing technological development to the poor, by means of technology resource and training centres situated in both rural and urban areas. Most importantly it is re-defined through understanding the links across social and environmental goals.

We are faced with social and environmental risks that can only be addressed through problem-solving approaches, which address multiple variables. Ontologically and epistemologically our discourses and perceptions of what constitutes research/ knowing have been shaped by the kind of teaching and research culture to which we have been exposed. The socio-political and economic environments we have experienced will limit our frames of reference unless we make a conscious effort to acknowledge diversity in our thinking. Once we understand the way in which society can and does shape knowledge we will be in a position to understand the shape of our perceptions and their implications for problem-solving. It is not my intention to blame people for being theoretically illiterate; this would be elitist. Power and knowledge are indeed linked, understanding how is the first step for emancipation.

If we believe the conclusions of sociologists, political scientists and economists, who argue that the state is now so unimportant that it can no longer shape the market and that essentially it is inevitable that the market will rule, we may become depressed and disempowered! If, however, we believe that structures can be shaped by the creative potential of human beings, we could argue that democracy and globalism could in fact be re-interpreted, as can citizenship. Democracy can be shaped through social movements that strive for an expanded sense of citizenship rights and responsibility, rather than an acceptance of the way things are.

The separation of private and public responsibility has ended in a bid to serve New Right interests. Through using the language of communitarianism in a way quite different from the way it was supposedly intended, individuals can be encouraged/sold the idea that groups of individuals, and not the state, are responsible for social and environmental justice. Once again an example of either/or thinking. Nevertheless, through social movements the new corporations could be steered to consider local (regional), national and international concerns through re-defining profit-taking into a global sense of citizenship based on shared risk and shared responsibility. This cultural shift will require re-education, according to Touraine (1995), because the ideologies of individualism and competition do not best serve the interests of global citizenship.

How can we help people to move from competitive to egalitarian thinking? The answer, which I try to develop in this book, is through using thinking tools to create shared webs of meaning.

Figure 1(a) is included in this chapter because it summarises the way in which we can see conflict and consensus either as useful co-definitions, or we can polarise conflict and consensus as being in quite different oppositional categories. Consensus and co-operation are vital for mutual survival. Conflict and adversarial thinking based on simplistic versions of Aristotelian categories, are the approaches that have driven capitalism to date.

But categories can also be perceived as part of a continuum or part of a dialogue because they exist in terms of each other. They define each other by their jigsaw relationship. Such an insight could help us to avoid the dangers of fragmented thinking that can have severe socio-political and economic repercussions. The Western philosophies, built on Aristotelian logic need to reconsider the continuums across phenomena rather than merely categorising phenomena into boxes, this requires forging webs of transcultural meanings. For instance, tools such as hyperlinks and overlays (based on lateral logic and webs) on the computer are as useful as categories and directories (based on binary oppositional logic and categories). Both and not 'either or' thinking is required for problem-solving for the new millennium.

Categories of knowledge help us to manage complexity and to specialise our knowledge, but they cannot help us to comprehend holistically. Specialisation is a double-edged sword. We could add to Foucault's (1967) maxim that not only 'power and knowledge' are linked but, instead, power, knowledge and culture are linked. Instead of thinking in terms of individual maps of meaning or group maps, we need to think in terms of global human maps and shared collaborative meaning, not competitive meaning.

Instead of responding to crises by developing explanations that somehow blame 'the other'—whether the other is an individual or particular category of people, who as a result of age, race, culture, politics or some other identifying characteristic can be singled out—tools can be used:

- to enhance the ability of global citizens to think creatively;
- to see the world through the lenses of all the stakeholders in specific social contexts;
- to comprehend the implications of values and assumptions on the way in which people define social problems; and
- to understand the logical flows between assumptions, values and their policy and practice implications.

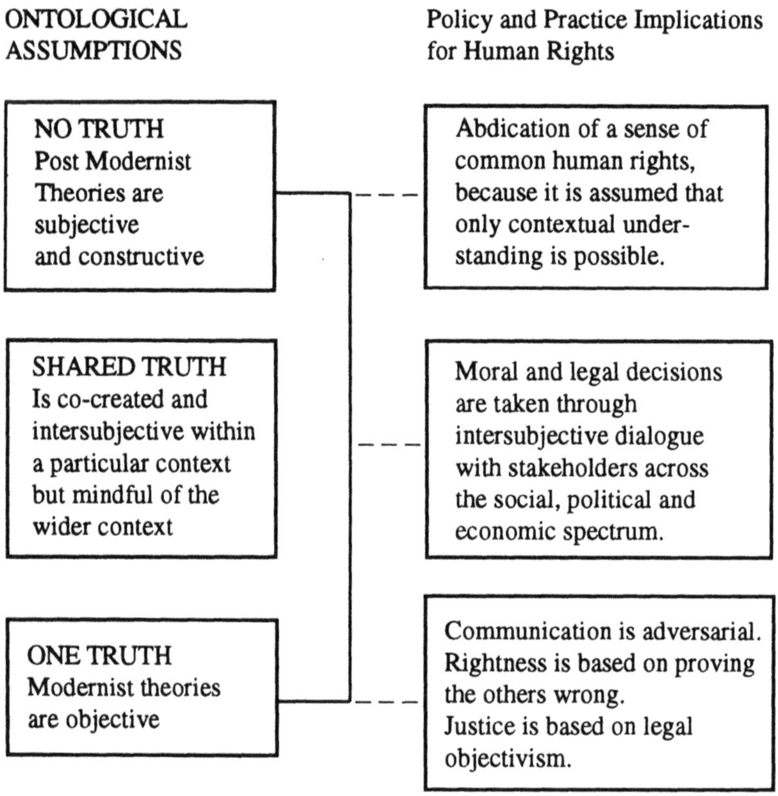

Figure 1a. Drawing together strands for a new shared sense of meaning. Source: McIntyre-Mills, 1988.

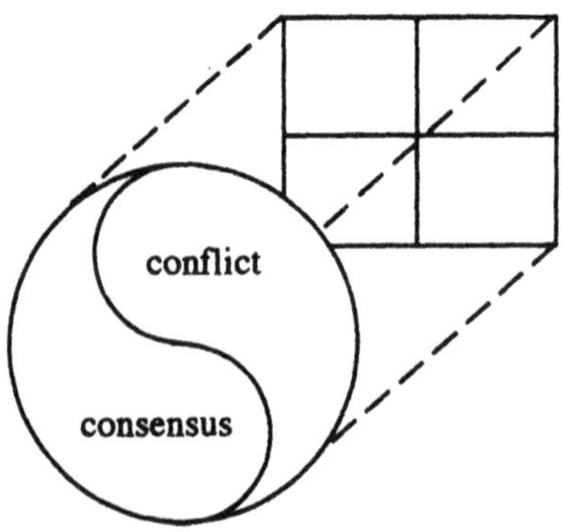

Figure 1b. Conflict and Consensus. Source: Brauer, 1996. Systems Practice 9(2):362.

Understanding needs to be contextual; we cannot pretend to come up with simplistic models, that can explain all things for all times. The best natural scientists understand the complexity of reality and that models are merely thinking tools and not blueprints that can be imposed. If we accept this sort of approach, then there is space for a revised sense of reliability and validity, in the sense that we need to compare texts and voices to find the overlaps and the differences. This is what interpolating across paradigms is about. Unfortunately, this requires either humility and an openness to other ideas or the desperation born of the realisation that existing models are no longer adequate!

Western thinking, according to Hettne (1995:188), has had a monopoly on "rational [categorical] thought" for centuries. He exhorts the reader to acknowledge the environmental, integrated contributions to thinking that have been made by indigenous peoples all over the world and by Eastern religions such as Buddhism, that advocate harmonious interplay amongst people, their environment and all living things. It is undeniable that, although these non-hierarchical thinking models contribute to systematic thinking, that they were often developed in very hierarchical social contexts.

Historically, sociological thinking had the chance to become systemic when Emile Durkheim drew on biological models to develop his functionalist explanations of society. Instead of developing holistic systemic thinking, the liberative potential of these early models was lost to the mechanistic versions of positivism. Instead of seeing cause and effect in biological terms that is in multiple, systemic feedback loops that we can understand more easily today as a result of cybernetics theory, cause and effect were seen in narrow mechanistic terms. The chance for humanistic thinking to be ecological was not grasped at that time, largely because complexity was so much more difficult to manage without complex computing tools.

A Note on Methodology

The book draws on fifteen years of multi-disciplinary, intersectoral and transcultural research. In addition, the statistics and arguments that have shaped the analysis are drawn from WHO and UN reports plus a host of other sources listed in the bibliography.

Introduction and Rationale for Book

> ...our culture teaches us not intellectual courage but intellectual conformity (Beer, 1974:20).
>
> No paradigm is hermetically sealed; the cracks provide the opportunity for enlightenment and change (Derivative, author unknown).

Thinking tools like technological tools are *not in themselves value neutral*. The design of a tool can in itself change the lives of the people who use it; for instance, time-keeping pieces and the assembly line made it possible to structure the working day in terms of "time is money" and to extract profit via surplus value. The implications for workers have been analysed by Braverman (1974), who described the degradation of work and de-skilling of workers and the value of a reserve army of labour. Mechanisation required passive workers to do compartmentalised work, but computerisation has arguably empowered (some) workers, who once again need to have analytical skills to programme computers. Computerisation, however, as yet has done nothing for the surplus worker, but, as argued below, could have considerable 'liberative potential' if used to enhance social movements for social justice. Creative linkages could be forged across interest groups that realise their common needs for social and economic survival. In the *public workspace* as much as in the *private domestic* space, technology has changed the life chances of some. For the affluent and working classes alike, in developed societies electrification and home gadgets have saved time and extended the opportunities of women, who have borne the brunt of domestic labour. Washing machines, ducted heating, microwaves and computers shape the life-style of privileged women who can now choose in some instances to work from home. The lack of this technology in less-developed societies and in developed societies amongst those who are without well-paid employment or **worse** without *access* to welfare leads to very different life chances, as United Nations (1991) statistics demonstrate.

Technology is an extension of the values of the designer; it is never value neutral. The polystyrene cup, paper plate and throw-away diaper are by no means value neutral; they tell us something about the designer's assumptions about the environment's capacity to be exploited and to absorb pollution.

It is worth bearing in mind, however, that no matter how carefully tools for thinking or doing are constructed, they can be colonised or taken over by those with other values and used for other purposes. It is therefore worth saying again that tools can be used to liberate and to oppress. Similarly, just because a set of ideas appears to be associated with a progressive individual, academic or community group, social movement, or political party, it is possible for these ideas to be used in many ways. Being aware of the context in which a model is being applied is essential if we are to enhance rather than retard democracy.

Liberative ideas can be colonised by autocrats and vice versa. For example: "self-help development" can be liberative or oppressive, depending on the system within which it is used. Governments bent on rationalising can 'window-dress' cutbacks in government spending in the name of 'self-help' or they can use self-help as a means to decentralise power. The values underpinning the concepts need to be unpacked and their implications unravelled. This is only possible if citizens are taught to think critically and creatively, rather than in terms of narrow frameworks. A thinking tool helps citizens to become aware of the policy implications of particular concepts. Ideas can be used for empowering the powerless and the powerful; understanding this is the first step towards liberation. Theories and methodologies need to be considered in terms of the ways in which they are used, rather than assuming that they are necessarily useful in all contexts. Contextual dialogue with all the stakeholders is vital. "Falsification" not "verification" is the basis for a sense of validity, as Popper (1968) has stressed. Popper did not use falsification in the iterative sense suggested by a paradigm-dialogue approach to check out meanings, but instead to define objective reality.

2

Intellectual Courage and Intellectual Conformity

> Ships of all kinds, for example, were instrumental in informing man (sic) of the vastness of his (sic) domain. They permitted different cultures to meet and cross-fertilise one another. The seafarer's ships and all his artefacts, his myths and legends, effectively translated his lore from generation to generation. And they transformed the unconscious of those who stayed on land as much as those who actually sailed (Weizenbaum, 1976:278).

Ships enabled people to cross oceans to discover 'what is on the other side'. Ships were invented in response to human need, imagination and curiosity. Thinking tools could also enable us to see the 'other side' of barriers created by simplistic models, and need to be invented as a necessity to understand a wider reality.

Transcultural tools could enable us to see interpolations across human maps. Cultural systems, which are disjointed, could be linked by finding shared lines of thinking. Human beings have maps that explain their own sense of reality or their ontology, for example, their sense of identity, destiny or place. When these are shaken by crises and the maps no longer explain reality, a sense of inner or interpersonal conflict occurs (Giddens 1995:193, 194).

The following vignettes aim to demonstrate that being well versed in sociological paradigms and understanding their political implications help to address social issues. Ontological and epistemological maps help locate perspectives and trace the contours or webs of meaning across constructs, rather than regarding positions of stakeholders as hermetically sealed paradigmatic boxes. Even paradigms, which are based on opposing assumptions, are created in dialogue with one another.

The vignettes give a sense of a personal journey away from intellectual conformity. During this journey windows were opened to other ways of making sense of the world. The same reality can be understood and/or constructed differently depending on one's willingness to be open to other ideas.

Contextualizing Socio-cultural Lenses: Transcultural Caring in Mental Health: An Exploration Using the Ethical Thinking Tool of 'Paradigm Dialogue'

As a researcher, I was asked to undertake a study of the different models of mental health and the way in which diagnoses are made in socio-political contexts. Power, knowledge and culture are closely linked in this case study.

At a hospital for the mentally ill in Cape Town, South Africa in the early 1980s, the frequent imposition of the definitions of "schizophrenia" led the head of psychiatry to wonder whether this diagnosis for the black Xhosa speakers was becoming increasingly prevalent. He requested that I research the rising trend, as he was not convinced that the diagnoses were 'correct'. He required a sociologist/social anthropologist to analyze the process of diagnosing (Mills, 1983, 1987a and b; McIntyre, 1995).

The diagnoses were made in the context of Apartheid South Africa where black, disenfranchised patients—the majority of whom were unemployed or underemployed in low-paid jobs—presented their symptoms to white, high-status, powerful English-speaking professionals who understood little or no Xhosa.

The patients' stories were translated by black, Xhosa-speaking nurses, who were perceived in the context of the hospital to be subordinate in the medical hierarchy to the psychiatrists. The professional hierarchy and the class and race hierarchy compounded the female nurses' perception that they needed to defer to the largely male 'seniors'.

Many nurses, however, by the same token perceived themselves to hold superior 'cultural capital' (in Bourdieu's sense, see Bourdieu and Wacquant, 1992), by virtue of their educational level, to the uneducated patients on whose behalf they mediated. In terms of African cosmology, 'intwaso' means that symptoms of illness and misfortune have been sent by their ancestors as 'a calling or a message'. The barrier between life and death is bridged by the ancestors who visit in dreams and through signs and symbols. The paradoxes and contradictions of life are patterned meaningfully through the cultural idiom of intwaso, which also provides a therapeutic route for sufferers. The diviner (igqira) interprets their dreams in the context of a ritual dance seance at which friends and family provide a rhythmic clapping and singing accompaniment. The search for healing often led patients to combine more than one therapeutic option (Janzen, 1978 and Mills, 1987a). Traditional cultural idioms were used as a vehicle for expressing their inability to cope and need to be understood, as such. Seeing ancestors in dreams and hearing their calling is not equivalent to schizophrenia, as the ethnocentric diagnoses of doctors indicated initially.

The construct of intwaso needed to be understood in terms of multiple paradigms, for instance:

(1) African illness cosmology *within the context of apartheid South Africa.*
(2) The cosmology of powerful, privileged white, Western biomedical practitioners, whose constructs of mental illness

were perceived as cultural capital as a result of their tertiary education. Their power gave them the right to downgrade African illness cosmology as myth and to represent 'the other' in terms of their privileged constructs.

(3) An understanding of the hierarchy of class and colour in Apartheid South Africa, which shaped the context of translations of symptoms by female black nurses for male white psychiatrists.

Learning about intwaso was a step away from what Bateson (1972) called simplistic or rote learning (Level 1). In this instance, from Western Colonial thinking and working critically only within one framework (Level 2 learning) towards Level 3 learning, which is holistic, interdisciplinary and transcultural, I had to re-think taken-for-granted notions of health, healing and perceptions of disease or misfortune and the therapeutic options and their possible combinations.

Thinking is bound to disciplinary bases and socio-political environments and these bases are used for defining competencies for practice. The lesson learned is that the compartmentalisation and the isolation of social problems lead to technocratic approaches to problem-solving. In this case prescribing drugs, albeit a necessary clinical response in some cases, without addressing the complex socio-political context in which mental illness occurs.

The Willingness to Share in Paradigm Dialogue is Not Equally Shared When Political Agendas Are at Stake

My second lesson was learned when I was asked to join the Safer Water and Sanitation Steering Committee in Pretoria, South Africa in 1986. It was set up long after the World Health Organisation's (WHO) Water Decade had been declared. The committee comprised members of the Council for Scientific and

Industrial Research, Department of Health and Welfare, Human Sciences Research Council (HSRC) and Department of Health. Not only was there competition amongst the paradigms of the professions—civil engineering, medicine and sociology / anthropology (Reason, 1991)—but considerable variation in political orientation. As the token, English-speaking female appointed because of my background in sociology and social anthropology and a member of HSRC staff, my perspective contrasted with a technocratic ontology, politically conservative ideas, and debased positivist notions of research epistemology (Reason, 1991). Let me explain each in turn.

Technocratic ontology

Concentrating on an effect of a problem such as poor water and seeing it *in isolation from the societal system* which produced it, and concentrating only on a *technological solution*—such as prescribing the construction of ferro cement tanks to catch rainwater in a rural area where there are no wealthy rate payers, rather than the construction of a costly dam—is an *economically and politically laden decision.*

Politically conservative ideas

Assuming that the state needs to be maintained not challenged, led most of the participants to ignore the fact that the WHO Decade had been declared years before the South African government decided to address the issue of safe water, or that the highest incidence of water and sanitation-related diseases overlapped with the so-called 'homeland' areas where black South Africans resided. By using sideways power, I networked beyond the committee to discuss public health paradigms with other academics who explored alternative academic and political paradigms with me (Mills, 1990 a and b).

Narrow, debased positivistic notions of research epistemology
Scientific humility depends on being open to all criticism of assumptions. The probability of 'truth' is based on failed attempts to falsify assumptions, not on narrow dogmatism. Openness to new ideas is a premise of post positivism.

Technocratic solutions, power plays across and within the social and natural sciences and the limitation of social responsibility were all part of this learning experience. The technological solution of implementing appropriate technology was explored dialogically with the stakeholders in a rural area of Boschfontein, where there was one of the highest incidences of typhoid in South Africa. Although water and sanitation-related diseases were undeniably major issues for all the people living in Boschfontein, these were seen by the local people to be on a par with unemployment and it made sense to them to use water and sanitation technology as a vehicle for job creation.

My contribution to this committee was to set up a demonstration project in Boschfontein, Kangwane. From the outset, action research methods were used to involve local residents in deciding how best to use a very limited amount of funding from the HSRC. Mindful that as Chambers (1983) said in his book *Rural Development: Putting the Last First* "research can be a mask for non action," I wanted to ensure that research would benefit some of the people, and not merely use the research as a whitewashing program and for my own postgraduate research.

It was clear from the start that local people in Boshfontein did not make up a homogenous group. Working out the interest groups and their particular constructs of how the health-related problem of typhoid should be addressed was my starting point. Identifying the interest groups and their overlapping and contradictory definition or construct of the problem was another entry point. Finding the common denominators amongst the groups was assisted by the nature of the problem. Everyone could see the advantage of collaboration to prevent illness. Some saw illness as a lower priority than addressing unemployment and the reason for the very different life chances of all South Africans. So the project had to be seen as a vehicle for addressing jobs and the empowerment of Boschfontein residents politically. Ferro-cement tanks and toilets were used as a vehicle for job creation, providing for basic water and sanitation needs, improving health, lobbying for political and policy reform.

A committee of representative residents (covering all interest groups) was set up to lobby Kangwane government on water and sanitation policy. In the process, a range of administrative, communication and technical skills were learned. This gloss should not give the impression that the project was without its share of problems. The biggest challenge was when I made the mistake of suggesting that instead of trying to keep the revolving fund going within the community to pay for materials (which when paid for could lead to the purchase of more) we apply for a grant from the Development Bank of Southern Africa (DBSA). People did not pay for the materials quickly and the fund became depleted despite 'top ups' by donations from the local bottleshop owner (in the interests of the community and his own credibility) and HSRC (in the interests of research and its own credibility).

Once the DBSA became involved 'the bottom up' participatory approach to development we had followed shifted away from the community base because the DBSA funds had to be channelled via the Kangwane government. The funding was a long time in coming and it took considerable lobbying by 'the some-what empowered' committee to get the funding earmarked for them to move out of homeland government coffers into the rural village. My credibility was on the line at this time and playing broker across the interest groups was a very exacting exercise of paradigm dialogue! Eventually some pipes were laid to connect KanGwane to a larger dam. This helped alleviate the dry-season water shortages and empowered local people politically. Further, the study was written up within a larger overview of the context of water and sanitation-related disease in rural areas in South Africa for the National Safer Rural Water and Sanitation Committee, and as chapters in academic works on development.

Construction of Reality and Rationalising Abusive Social Policy

The most passionately felt lesson came about as a result of working with homeless children aged from 8 to 18 years in Pretoria, South Africa in 1988-1989. The notion of talking to people with completely different frameworks was thrown into stark reality when I approached the social workers from the Transvaal Provincial Administration, who informed me that there were "no street children in Pretoria". When I explained that I was currently working with many children who were homeless, I was informed that these children were not South African citizens and were not therefore part of their jurisdiction or concern. Similarly, when members of the committee discussed with local police the children's rights to safety and (at the very least) their right to earn a living in the absence of any social welfare, the notions of childhood, rights, work and welfare were constructed very differently. The assumptions and values underpinning these constructs were central to passionate discussions. Dialogue attempted to demonstrate the ethical implications of definitions, which denied rights to some young people by virtue of the way in which they were classified by immoral government statutes.

Working in a team with like-minded people across a range of disciplines led to the formation of a committee and network called Street-Wise, Pretoria. This committee and network aimed to provide for the immediate needs of young people who were homeless, to research the problem and to lobby for their rights. Pretoria-Street-Wise is now part of a national organisation. In 1988–1989 when the project was set up, the challenge of working across the stakeholders can be epitomised by a workshop that police, so-called welfare workers, academics and a lawyer for human rights attended. Identifying assumptions of stakeholders and understanding their implications was essential. By asking participants for definitions of 'work', 'welfare' and 'childhood' and exploring their implications for practice, some participants were able to identify implications of their values, contradictions amongst them, and the links between their assumptions and practice.

Action Research, Trialing Thinking Tools for Systemic Development in Rural Samar

The Philippines is one of the poorest Asian countries, with a population of 70 million. Northern Samar, Eastern Philippines, is one of the poorest provinces, with great ecotourism potential if the coconut palms are not over-exploited for copra and the coral reefs are not decimated by dynamite fishing.

As a visitor I was perceived in many ways, for example, as a teaching resource to help the colleges, technicons and universities I visited gain further accreditation. Hence, my activities were documented by means of photographs for the education authorities. Local academics also were able to benchmark their subject content on development studies against my input at undergraduate and postgraduate levels. Further, I was seen as a possible problem-solver of development challenges.

'Stranger value' can allow one the opportunity to share novel processes for teaching and development which may not be shared easily if you are "merely a local". At a two-day conference called 'Lessons from the Field', the expectations of the wide range of delegates representing academia, government and nongovernment were challenged. Instead of learning passively from the 'so-called foreign expert,' who was heralded with considerable hype in the form of banners (which I hasten to add are quite normal for so-called dignitaries, 'foreign or otherwise'), the seminar involved not only traditional lectures but divergence of the large group into small focused group discussions on one of six development sectors, panel presentations by group representatives, discussion and questioning from the floor ,and the setting up of a committee drawn from the participants.

The assumption which I discussed at the outset were:

(1) Social justice could be better served by thinking in terms of interlocking sectors or overlapping, connected circles impacting on development arenas.
(2) Tools for integrated development thinking could be useful to facilitate problem-solving. The goal of thinking tools is not merely to solve problems, but to understand the nature of problems—in other words, to understand problems in terms of the ramifications of their social, political and economic complexity. By questioning the taken-for-granted, we can ascertain who defines a set of circumstances as a problem and why; a problem to one interest group could be of no concern to some or a solution to another. *We need to develop models which are not just static aggregations of data but dynamic systems which are based not on statistical averages but also on qualitative data which represents the complexity of reality* (Beer, 1974:38).

Delegates were grouped in terms of political, economic and socio-cultural (health, education, leisure) sectors. My role as facilitator was to help delegates understand the systemic links within and amongst the sectors. Focus group discussions are

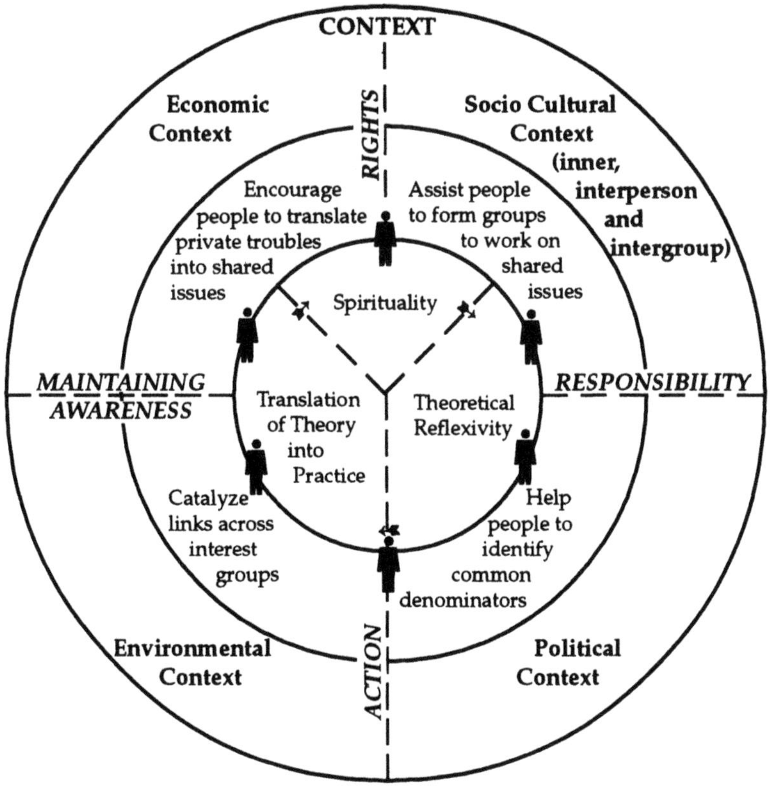

Figure 2. A Mandala for helping us think about the complexity of each situation. Source: Adapted from Hancock and Perkins, Dept. of Public Health, City of Toronto, Canada: 60.

vital for pooling knowledge and opinions about development issues, provided they are conducted with knowledge of the social, political and economic context of the research. It is naive to imagine that people will feel free to communicate openly if they feel in any way threatened by fellow participants with multiple agendas.

To begin, a lecture on 'styles of thinking and learning' set the scene. Three styles of learning were outlined, from rote learning, to the application of single frameworks and then to the use of reflexive thinking, requiring multiple frameworks as identified by Bateson (1972).

The members of the seminar were requested to do the following tasks with the aid of thinking tools. The first task was to *describe their sector* using quantitative as well as qualitative data that would be helpful, as the latter includes emotions, opinions and attitudes essential for understanding development needs. The second task was to *describe successful community development projects* in their sector and the third to *describe their vision for their sector*. We discussed the difference between *reflective*[4] *approaches* used in counselling, with which some of the participants were familiar, and *reflexive thinking*—by means of the analogy of different coloured lenses. I drew up sets of lenses with blue, purple, red and green lenses on large sheets of paper and shared how 'the colour of our lenses' could filter the way in which we see or define social problems. The blue symbolised systemic thinking; the purple, feminist thinking; the red, conflict thinking; and the green, ecological thinking. In day-to-day working life, our assumptions and values filter out some colours in favour of others. Understanding requires mapping out the point of view of the 'other'.

The seminar ended with the analogy that if one arranged the lenses (symbolic of basic models for thinking) into a 'stained-glass window of options,' this would help one to see the world in a different light. This analogy struck a deep chord in the largely Christian environment, where church windows and icons are sacred tools for reflection.

The tasks attempted to help participants explore development challenges through considering the implications of adhering to a particular set of assumptions. The participants were asked to work in focus groups, one per sector, in order to complete the tasks and apply group norms to ensure the best dynamics for participation.

All six groups applied the thinking tools to local development initiatives. For some the exercise posed few challenges because the concept of critical thinking was quite familiar. For others, the shift from thinking only in terms of some of the lenses was new and not a little strange. The suggestion that these tools could be useful for problem-solving across interest groups was disputed by two participants who said that the only solution was to spell out that "one was opposed to corruption, fight it and own the label of rebel or subversive thinker". One participant was quite annoyed by the notion that thinking tools could help people to find common denominators in order to make collaboration across interest groups possible. At the time, a civil war raged with Muslim rebels who were considered beyond the pale by some of the workshop participants. The term 'collaboration or collaborative dialogue' has very strong political overtones of being 'a traitor' or merely pragmatic. 'Co-creation through dialogue' is a better concept for explaining the notion of finding 'the liberative potential' (Gouldner, 1980) within many paradigms, or interpolating across paradigms (Flood and Romm, 1996; Thurow, 1996) and using ideas creatively through paradigm dialogue.

All four lessons confirmed the assumption that power and knowledge are linked, but knowledge can be reconstructed through action research. These experiences show that: 1) individual perceptions need to be considered contextually within social, historical, political and economic structures; 2) private troubles need to be contextualized; and 3) action research can serve the democratic empowerment of the socially and politically marginalised.

Stimulating intellectual dexterity is essential if we wish to: 1) forge transcultural webs of meaning; 2) interpolate across different maps of meaning; and 3) weave a common tapestry from the different strands of experience.

3

Tools for Transcultural Ethical Thinking

Reflection helps to draw out the positive aspects of our own and the other's thinking:

> Criticism is a relatively easy form of intellectual achievement and much used by mediocre minds who are unable to be creative or constructive. . . Intellectualism has deservedly got a bad reputation. It is possible to play logical word games in which one concept generates another in a sort of virtuoso ballet of ideas. . . Traditionally thinking has been in the form of debate, clashes and polemics. This has arisen from our dependence on dialectics as the only form of developmental thinking. This new process of 'exlectics' seeks to draw out and improve what is good in an idea rather than to attack what is bad. . . Because philosophers have largely been involved in word games or mathematical games, logic has come to assume a dominant position in thinking. In practice when we are thinking about the real world rather than some artificially constructed world of words or numbers, perception is very much more important than logic. . . (De Bono, 1977:68-70)

As an academic and practitioner, schooled in social anthropology and sociology, I feel bound to ask:

- How can we avoid technocratic thinking which leads us to assume that a set of rules for thinking and action can encompass all the possibilities?

- How can citizens learn to think critically and analytically to avoid rigid thinking that could lead to misguided action?
- How can we teach and learn compassion that flows from understanding the point of view of another person?

The big questions have an impact at the coalface of human service delivery. The challenge that we have to address as so-called professionals in welfare services is: How can we ever hope to help people if we ration out empathy according to time limits of an interview or the mission statement of a service organisation geared to cost-cutting? These are some of the issues that have concerned service providers. Working in transcultural contexts with people accustomed to being "given plenty of time," because time is not equated with money in less-developed contexts, merely serves to highlight the problem. We need to explore connections between private troubles and public issues, but we need theoretical literacy, skills and strategies to achieve this end in the context of the eroded welfare state. In this environment, caregivers can become driven to meet the demands of the marketplace and to learn marketable skills; welfare service agencies are driven to adopt competency procedures, that provide blueprints which undermine creative thinking and practice. The normative competency approach put forward by Wolfensburger (1980, 1983, 1989, 1991) in numerous publications and seminars on "social role valorisation" thrives in this environment and teaches students and practitioners to adopt technocratic, simplistic approaches to intervention and evaluation. This approach and ones like it are more insidious than they appear at first; they encourage practitioners to become passive service providers who do not make policy or practice contributions and instead remain passive consumers of what the market dictates.

We need thinking tools to help us:

(1) Unpack the way in which we select concepts (often on the basis of what is in favour and by definition what constitutes knowledge);
(2) Re-define concepts; and
(3) Unravel their implications for policy and practice by using them in PAR (Participatory Action Research). PAR is cyclical, rather than linear. Unlike traditional research that strives to ascertain answers through expert power, PAR strives to draw out the lived experiences and perceptions of all the participants. PAR attempts to: a) learn by doing or more specifically by implementing real changes in specific contexts, and b) achieve processes of iterative feedback amongst all the participants.

Technology and Thinking Tools

Let's reconsider technology and thinking tools. As human beings we have undergone vast shifts in the way we think, from invoking magic in pre-scientific times as a way of dealing with the unmanageable and explaining away the unpredictable. Later, religion provided the major source of explanation in life and provided a set of guidelines for living and thinking. Western science in particular provided an alternative set of explanations based on a so-called rational understanding of the laws of nature, which, if understood could enable the scientist to dominate, control and mould nature to the needs of 'mankind'. The language of scientific domination is aggressive and masculine in its archetypal idiom. As science developed so did the realisation that Western models based on a mechanistic notion of cause and effect were not sufficiently sophisticated to explain complex, weblike feedback links amongst variables. Simplistic models did not suffice. The exploits of the developed world have led to unexpected outcomes.

As Ulrich Beck (1992) has stressed, we now live in a world where we do not feel that we can control everything on the basis of current Western rationalism, because the risks we face now are not only "seen" but "unseen." Linear thinking and "either or thinking" continue to be the mainstays of Western thinking and problem-solving. Argument is geared at disproving the point of view of "the other." Further, a sense of nihilism as much as a sense of humility has driven postmodernism.

Poststructuralism is healthier in so far as ensuring that simplistic models are not claimed to be representations of what is recognised to be a more complex, messy and paradoxical world, thanks to fuzzy set theory and chaos theory, for instance. Eastern philosophies such as Taoism and Buddhism, which emphasised the harmonious interplay between yin and yang, and the way in which one category defines the other, and the paradoxical nature of reality, seem to have more meaning to the Western mind as a sense of humility dawns. But in many quarters, as voices of the other who criticise the dominant academic paradigms are increasingly heard, there is a hardening of the voice of the dominant paradigm in response to market pressures. It is this hardening or ossifying of which we need to be watchful, if we are to continue to create webs of meaning and, in the process, a sense of global citizenship and shared destiny.

Unlike Crook, Pakulski and Waters (1993:67), it can be argued that McLuhan and Powers' (1989) work is not utopian in its support of postmodernism. McLuhan and Powers are aware that changes, whether technological or social, have potential strengths and weaknesses. Our challenge as global citizens is to maximise our strengths and minimise our weaknesses when bringing about changes. Being able to see paradoxes is the first step. Insights can be facilitated by means of some of the thinking tools, such as tetrad or triple loop learning, explained below.

> . . .McLuhan prefigures the theme of a 'distracted' postmodern audience when he argues that television discourages intense, linear involvement. Television re-integrates the senses and establishes a regime of experience which is mosaic rather than linear, iconographic rather than perspectival. . ." (Crook et al., 1993:67, 68).

By presenting ideas as images and speaking in quick soundbites, we may get a sense that we understand what is happening as a result of looking at TV news 'on the box,' which frames what happens in the global village. But media ownership dictates what constitutes news and the frame delimits what is acceptable and what is not. Power shapes cultural perceptions and what constitutes knowledge. What constitutes news is followed by advertising that uses symbols of the global village.

This is the theme taken by Baudrillard (1983, in Crook et al., 1993:68): "Media technologies become complicity in the erosion of distinctions between representation and reality, surface and depth, leaving an immanent surface where operations unfold—a smooth operational surface of communication". They go on to quote Baudrillard's work, which argues that Disneyland—a reflection of the imaginary world made real in a circumscribed area—meets the need for people to believe in the fantasy of the medium. Disneyland and "The News" as interpreted by the powerful are at times equally fantastic. Other fantasies for children and distractions for adults provide an antidote to the reality of poverty and social marginalisation. Television is the modern equivalent of the Roman policy of "bread and circuses" for the masses. Although with cutbacks to the welfare state, the "*basic needs*" for the masses may not be addressed as much as the *fantasies* for the masses!

Some academic thinkers have started to encourage the use of thinking tools to help shift human beings away from simplistic thinking. These academic thinkers are of course standing on the shoulders of many earlier religions and philosophies!

As we become influenced by global communications, the communication medium shapes the content of the message and, to use McLuhan and Powers' (op. cit.) play on words, in a sense 'massages' our way of thinking. Simplistic rather than complex messages are emphasised in the media and we have a greater sense of alienation from the problems of the world beamed into our homes. News of wars, famines, political elections becomes soap opera, but complex messages abound in the advertising media. McDonalds's advertises a world of "Mac Time" community where, across the world, food could taste the same at mealtime (Kincheloe and McLaren, in Burkett, 1996). This sense of community is based on a multi-national company encouraging the spread of a fast food mass culture (op. cit.).

In schools we need to teach children to think analytically and creatively, not merely competitively "to get good jobs" and "to succeed' in terms of the narrow profit motive. What hope is there that this can be achieved as governments cut back on educational services and privatisation increases? Can teachers and children think independently at schools and tertiary institutions funded by corporations? These are questions that have a central bearing on democracy and ethics. As long as the market economy approach predominates in the world, we need to use our ability as consumers to decide what political parties, companies and agencies we will support or boycott. We have to decide how to shape the world through active global citizenship. This involves both thinking and action to ensure that social justice gains are maintained or that social injustices are addressed through wide-ranging social movements. Each global citizen needs to become aware of his or her rights and responsibilities.

The work of Pierre Bourdieu (1987; with L. J. D. Wacquamt, 1992) is useful for understanding cultural capital within social contexts and the way in which different classes interpret their reality, but it does not provide any details about how to bring about social change. Nor does his work address the reality that despite class differences and the differences in cultural capital, we are in fact all the custodians of one ecosystem. His concepts "field", "strategy" and "habitus" are useful in so far as he uses them to veer away from bald structure to the messy, complex reality in which people live and interpret their lives. The way in which he places personal biography of the intellectual within the context of social research is also invaluable. He does not believe that reflexivity is about reflecting on the life of the researcher and the researched as a dyad. Instead, he looks at the habitus and field of both and through 'strategy' introduces the notion of power. In this sense he is different from other reflexive theorists such as Giddens, and is useful in so far as he places a sense of responsibility in the hands of each social thinker.

The goal of thinking tools is not merely to solve problems, such as cutbacks in welfare services, education and health, but to understand the nature of problems holistically in the sense of questioning the "taken for granted" and asking: Who defines a set of circumstances and phenomena as a problem and why? A problem to one interest group could be a solution to another. The notion that problems can be solved through competition for so-called "scarce resources" has been the hallmark of history.

To help solve problems with "the other," we have to realise that the definitions of problems and solutions are based on deeply held assumptions about the world (Geddes, in Geddes, Hughes and Remenyi, 1994). Within cultures, gender, age, personal and material resources can be ascribed very different meanings. The challenge for global citizens is, on the one hand, to develop or retain right-hemisphere, lateral and holistic thinking without resorting to postmodern doubt and, on the other hand, to realise that the social world is more complex than was previously represented in neat, structural models that characterise left-hemisphere, modern thinking.

If we can understand that the closest we can ever get to a shared sense of 'truth' is through listening to and understanding the frame of reference of the other, then the first step will be taken. Ideally democracy is about exploring conceptual boundaries and overlaps amongst people in order to address power imbalances and to attempt to restore harmony within them and their environment. The life chance links between health and development in terms of physical, mental and spiritual well-being have received increased recognition in recent years as a result of the official ratification of the World Health Organisation beginning with the Ottawa Health Charter of 1986. These links have long been understood in societies where modern positivistic science does not channel thinking into rigid compartments.

Thinking tools to help us map out the constructs of participants are vital, because essentially that is what democratic development is about—negotiation of meanings through dialogue, in order to restore social and environmental imbalances (Ife, 1995). Often this means changing the existing balance of power. Dialogue requires an ability to read and record the constructs of stakeholders so that the social action is taken is perceived to be appropriate by the "have-nots" and is likely to get as many of the "haves" on theirside as possible! As Participatory Action Researchers we try to empower others to act for themselves but we also act as advocates. We give voice to others by couching their needs and perceptions in the language, themes and idioms of the powerful and culturally dominant. In this sense the powerful can take away their voice and downgrade the value of their knowledge. Not all Indigenous knowledge is empowering to all stakeholders, but as researchers we need to be aware of the role we play in representing and silencing ideas within particular contexts. An ongoing dialogue ensures better representation of a spectrum of voices.

There is more at stake operating at the interpersonal level than mere egotism and ethnocentrism, if the ecosystem is to survive. Advances in technological thinking have not as yet been accompanied by advances in socio, cultural and ethical thinking. Skilled workers may be efficient in so far as they achieve the goals of the organisation, but whether they achieve effective or desirable change as far as all the stakeholders are concerned, is debatable. De Bono talks of "proto truths" rather than "absolute truth". He acknowledges the constructs of stakeholders and strives to work out negotiated, shared proto truths or constructs within particular contexts. He also assumes that a decision, that undermines the rights of another with disregard for his humanity, is a perversion of the process. This striving for a shared sense of truth he calls a "kind of hypothesis testing" (1977). Social justice in the public sphere and care in the private sphere (Gilligan, 1982 and Larrabee, 1993) can be better served by connectedness and lateral thinking rather than "either or thinking."

Organic thinking based on what De Bono (1993) calls "water logic" assists us to make organic representations of thinking. Techniques such as this can help us to avoid the narrow dogma of "I am right and you are wrong" (De Bono 1993) or the notion of thinking in terms of simplistic binary oppositions to use the words of Levy-Strauss (1987). The ability to see the logical flow or 'flowscape' (De Bono 1993) from particular sets of assumptions to particular conclusions is an imperative for breaking existing moulds of thinking and acting. This is a useful tool for needs assessment, project planning, participatory management, conflict resolution and evaluation.

Exploring boundaries and overlaps amongst people in order to address power imbalances is essential in order to attempt to restore harmony within them and their environment. An approach, that reflects on the implications of the various sets of assumptions avoids the extremes of individualism and collectivism.

How can these webs of common meaning be forged? Transcultural thinking tools that emphasise the rights and responsibilities of global citizens who can engage in 'both and' thinking are vital for setting up inclusive social movements. The work of Touraine (1995) and Castells (1996–8) stresses that social movements rather than class movements are the political strategies most appropriate for the new millennium. Bourdieu (1987; with L. J. D. Wacquant, 1992) argues that the vehicle for bringing about change is through cultural re-education, and that individuals and groups need to take responsibility in their everyday lives to shape changes in the way they think and act in their private and public capacities.

The face of welfare and development is changing but social action can play a role in maintaining and regaining rights and responsibilities. The most marginalised groups are discriminated against in terms of demographic and mental/physical characteristics (age, gender, intellectual and physical capacity measured in terms of specific criteria or so-called racial characteristics), socio-cultural considerations (religious or party affiliations), economic-class, or status considerations.

Webs of meaning can be created through finding common denominators across interest groups. Only when people can be persuaded to see that they have interests in common with others can global citizenship be achieved. Helping groups and individuals make the connections is a starting point, but knowledge, understanding and behaviour are not necessarily linked. This is the challenge. In every sphere of life, knowing does not provide the will to change behaviour. But the will does come from the desire for self- or group preservation. So there is hope for collaboration and cooperation when the whole of the human race sees that it is in its interest to do so. Paradoxically, human beings need to be both independent and part of a group

(Berger, 1977); these are two competing needs that are shaped culturally to be dominant or almost absent in some contexts. Independence and competition are more acceptable in some western cultural contexts than in many Eastern, African, American and most Australian Aboriginal cultural contexts, for example. Without being naively simplistic, we need to interpolate the thinking tools of so-called developed, competitive societies with the thinking tools of so-called less-developed, collaborative societies. Both styles of thinking assist human survival in specific contexts and have much to teach the 'other' but, more importantly, the shared areas need to be acknowledged and explored. This is the challenge.

For instance, explanations that blame the natural versus the non-natural for illness and misfortune occur in both developed and less-developed societies. Religion and mysticism exist side by side, with explanations rooted in what passes for 'science'. Western thinking could benefit by exploring the ideas of interconnectedness in explanations of health and illness.

Some thinking tools will be presented that help to address the subject/researcher barrier sometimes referred to as the emic/outsider versus etic/insider barrier. We can avoid the issue by simply acknowledging that emotions shape our findings and that we are "part of our own subject matter", as stressed by Habermas, Giddens and many other critical and reflexive thinkers. Instead, we can strive towards empathy and faithful constructions through the use of dialogue aided by some tools for mapping constructs. African indigenous healers, for example, deal with and erase the barrier of 'self' and 'other' simply by insisting that one cannot heal others until one has suffered and recovered so that one can feel the pain of 'the other'. Tools can, however, be used to enhance one's ability to see the world through the lenses of all the stakeholders in specific social contexts. Theoretical literacy is a response to a postmodernist reality of competing constructs of "truth". The Japanese name the white space in a picture. If we ignore this contextual space, we miss much of the picture. When communicating we need to be constantly aware of this figure/ground nexus, what is said is equally important as what is unsaid.

What are tools for thinking? Thinking tools help to shift us from thinking in simplistic binary oppositions. They help us to see the point of view of the other. We use thinking tools to see the world of the other and to represent it faithfully; to assist the illiterate and innumerate to represent themselves to achieve a measure of social justice and to find common strands of meaning; not to force our frame of reference on the other but to comprehend, respect and find common denominators by virtue of our shared humanity.

Triple Loop Learning: A Liberative Tool for 'Both and Thinking'

Triple Loop Learning, a critical systems tool, could help the user make connections across a host of variables and undertake complex problem-solving in a range of areas, rather than encouraging the isolation of single causes for complex problems. In the television news media, in particular, there has been a tendency to come up with fragmented analyses and compartmentalised solutions to complex problems. The Triple Loop learning tool can be applied to a range of organisational and social movement contexts. We need to take the time to apply it in the quest to reduce the harm in the world that results from "either or thinking".

This tool contributes to a critical movement to establish holistic thinking. Flood and Romm question the taken-for-granted assumptions anchored within paradigms, which can lead to 'mind traps' (Vickers, cited by Flood and Romm, 1996:129). They discuss ways to move away from working within narrow 'centres of learning' to holistic systems thinking which, to extract from and paraphrase Flood and Romm, concentrate on:

- "What" questions, such as "are we doing the right things?" This is about making decisions based on exploring the meanings people attribute to decisions.
- "How" questions, such as "are we doing things right?", and
- "Why" questions, about the political context of decision making or what they call "might-right questions".

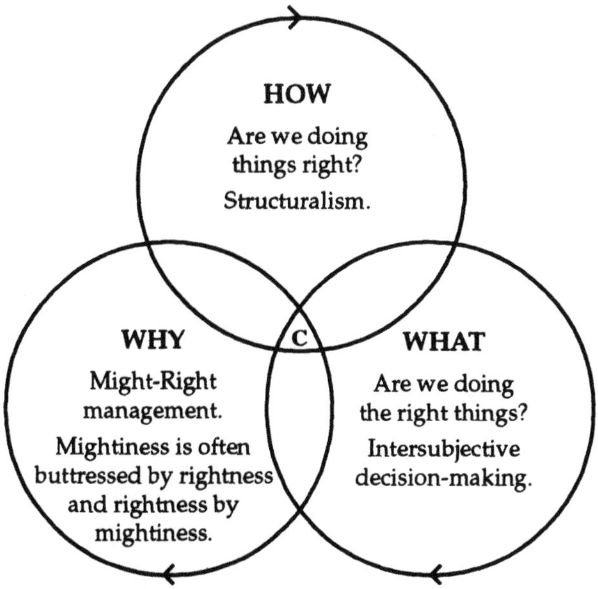

Figure 3. Loops of Learning. Source: Flood & Romm (1996:xiii, fig. P).

In a Venn diagram, they show the overlaps amongst all three domains of learning to remind us of their conceptual interconnectedness.

> A critical view (that underpins triple loop learning) states that hybridisation may be carried out in conjunction with explicit reasoning about the purpose and principles in play. Choice must be made about the form of the hybrid, the (main) purpose that is to be pursued, and the principles therefore that have to be followed. Choice is not once-and-for-all time however. Choice in the critical

> scheme of things will be revisited and may change. . . Any set of rules may be rational or expedient only for one set of actors (Gouldner, 1954:18). And there may be many sets of concerns of actors within any organisation. This is where the importance of debate surfaces. Debate is an important part of the process whereby people's decision making becomes increasingly well informed in terms of the other people's concerns. . ." (Flood and Romm, 1996:111).

By interpolating across the domains of ontological and epistemological maps of diverse discourses, instead of proliferating yet another paradigm, an effort is made to create common ground or "common denominators" (McIntyre, 1995) on 'maps'. Rather than engaging in debate leading to proliferation, it is advocated that commensurable points of overlap could be found that could in turn lead to the drawing together of knowledge which has been previously discipline-bound. The discipline bound approach attempts to prove one perspective right by disproving another's perspective. This is a result of thinking in 'either/or terms' rather than 'both/and' terms. De Bono calls this an exegetic process or an attempt to find proto truths (1977); Gouldner (1980) calls it trying to find the 'liberative potential' in theories. McLuhan and Powers (1989) refer to this as tetradic thinking (McIntyre, 1996). Romm and Flood have applied their reflexive thinking to deriving a creative tool called Triple Loop Learning, which summarises the debates about critical thinking, the contextual, constructed nature of knowledge, and the bid to manage diversity by creating commensurable interpolations of discourses across disciplines. Triple Loop Learning enables us to avoid polarising modernism and postmodernism, and instead to explore the overlaps, gaps and potentials of discourses by asking the three above-mentioned main questions.

This Critical Systems Theory called Triple Loop Learning tool stresses the need to avoid the bigoted isolationism of working narrowly within one box-like paradigm, or the cynicism of merely importing concepts from another paradigm and colonising them so as to make the old paradigm palatable to a wider audience. The danger of course being that the concepts start to mean different things when defined in terms of other sets of assumptions. 'Pragmatism' is about an 'eclectic mix' based on trial and error and 'complementarism' is about 'reflexive eclecticism' geared at finding appropriate "grounds for comparison".

Romm and Flood's (1996) goal is to provide a tool to challenge power bases. In this sense they harness the liberative potential of postmodern theory and avoid the ethical nihilism of "there is no truth". It can be argued that the closest we can get to truth is through intersubjective dialogue within a specific social, political and economic context with all the stakeholders of an ethical decision. There are no blueprints for decision-making (McIntyre, 1995). But this does not mean that the principle of social justice is undermined. Romm and Flood exhort citizens to use liberative thinking tools to rid the world of paradigms that support "power over" people and instead support "power to" people.

The basic assumption underpinning the approach to learning is that instead of seeing the world through a single lens—by bringing a spectrum of lenses together into a stained-glass window and standing back, the implications of seeing the view in terms of one lens as opposed to many become a little more comprehensible and open up a diversity of ontological considerations.

It would be naive to deny that Triple Loop Learning using a range of group working, collaborative and participatory research methodologies and methods geared at emancipation can occur when there is no political will. Flood and Romm (1996) quote Quine and Ulian (1978...25): "Webs of belief can be respun to account for supposed evidence. The credibility of the positivist idea of using evidence as a way of testing theory was therefore strongly challenged by Quine". One could argue that if we agree with this and with Habermas (1974) that we are all part of our subject matter and that our assumptions colour the way in which we make sense of the world even when we do the most carefully designed and controlled research. Why should this tool help us to avoid the trap? Perhaps the only answer is that at least Triple Loop Learning and other thinking tools provide a means to question our conclusions, rather than accepting them as dogmatic blueprints that allow powerful decision-makers to decide what is best for 'the other' on the basis of the scientific proof of "the experts".

If research is participatory and based on collaboration, there is still plenty of scope for abuse of power. In groups, powerful personalities can dominate; in transcribing ideas they can be misinterpreted or taken out of context. Iterative feedback can help to alleviate this and, if the full diversity of opinion is noted, the challenge to find the general rule can be offset by the challenge to find space for the exceptions to the rule (McIntyre 1996). If this can be achieved by using thinking tools such as Triple Loop Learning, then it could help to make a contribution to maintaining the balance between collectivism and individualism—which is the dilemma with which democracy is always faced (Berger, 1977; and Touraine, 1995).

The ever-present challenge is the human paradox of wanting to be an individual and needing to be accepted within a collective. The theories that have addressed this paradox can be 'mapped out' ontologically. In line with 'either/or thinking' geared at promoting one academic thinker at the expense of the other, debates have raged between consensus or conflict thinkers. Postmodernism has provided a positive contribution to these debates by arguing that there is no truth. The downside of this argument is, however, the way in which it can be used politically to adopt a nihilistic approach to a shared sense that social justice is possible. But what does social justice mean? By virtue of our humanity, we all have needs—albeit met in culturally specific ways. Extreme relativism can lead to a denial of any shared sense of needs and behavioural responsibilities that are beyond the pale. The danger of extreme forms of postmodernism is that is does not have a normative component. Poststructuralism appears to have more liberative potential (particularly when considered with less extreme forms of postmodernism), in that it accepts that the world is messy and complex and that neat structures do not provide the full story.

Similarly the methodologies that have been used to do research have been geared to non-objectivism, or understanding the constructs and objectives geared to finding solutions and the big picture. Methodological thinkers such as Ian Dey (1993) have argued that the 'either or thinking' or one approach is better than the other is misplaced because methods suited to answering questions about number and meaning can be combined in designs suited to addressing a particular problem.

Ethical issues such as the means (process) and ends (outcomes) that confront global citizens can be addressed by means of thinking tools, so that students and practitioners are aware of the implications of their assumptions (explicit and implicit) for their own practice. The issues of privacy, anonymity, responsibility, sincerity, so-called professional expertise; the issues of representation in research, humility and willingness to learn from the experience of 'the other' can be addressed through theoretical and methodological literacy. Learning to think through the implications of where we situate ourselves on "maps" will help us to develop ethical practice. The closest we can come to a sense of shared "truth" is through dialogue with all the participants who are affected by a decision. It is rooted in the reflection on possibilities and an awareness of the structures of power. In this sense it "retrieves" (McLuhan and Powers, 1989) Popper's approach to knowledge, based on attempts to falsify propositions but "obsolesces" (op cit.) the rigidity of its objectivism.

Authors who understand the links across disciplines and whose work cannot be pigeon-holed include De Bono (1977; 1993), Bourdieu (1987; with Wacquamt, 1992), Bateson (1972), Giddens (1991; 1995), Touraine (1995), Flood and Romm (1996), Foucault (1967; with Gordon, 1980), Orlando Fals-Borda and M. A. Rahman (1991) and Freire (1982). Their works, which despite many differences, have in common a holistic grasp of the links amongst variables (irrespective of disciplines). They are all on the same track in this respect and have laid the foundations for creating common ground across disciplinary boundaries and the basis for theoretical and methodological literacy. At first glance the above thinkers appear to be a strange melange. De Bono is a social psychologist whose work has been applied to solving a host of problems ranging from the micro level of the individual and group concerns in private and public domains to wider issues, which the newly formed De Bono Institute for World Thinking in Melbourne, Australia is beginning to consider—albeit from a largely business perspective.

We need problem-solving techniques suited to the social and natural world, to educational institutions at every level, business and human service environments, and this requires holistic or multi-semic thinking. Maturana and Verela (1973, 1980) should be added to this list because their work is based on the premise that the world is an interacting system, and they eschewed the notion of separate categories or disciplines separating knowledge. Stafford Beer (1973) made this a key point of his foreword to their book *Autopoiesis: The Organization of living*. However, Mingers (1995) in his book *Self-producing Systems: Implications and Applications of Autopoiesis* appears to abandon the notion of knowledge being one system and instead creates separate iron maidens of a number of disciplines. Each of these, he argues, is self-sustaining rather than seeing the disciplines as necessarily part of one overall system.

Giddens' (1984) notion of structuration theory, which in essence explains how structures influence thinking and social action and vice versa, uses this insight to elaborate what he calls 'the double hermeneutic'. The contextuality of all knowledge within time and space is spelled out with a refreshing emphasis on thinking, feeling actors who inhabit human bodies. Anthropology and sociology are linked in his endeavours. He sees the social researcher as part of his or her own subject matter. The webs of meaning between the researcher and other are linked.

This essay does not attempt to make a pretentious new contribution to theory or methodology, but instead tries to underline the achievements that have already been made in the direction of synthesis. Like Hegel's dialectic which he applied specifically to history, **knowledge** can be seen to progress through thesis, antithesis and synthesis. Thinking tools used intersubjectively to help us see knowledge in terms of the various stakeholder's perceptions will help us achieve synthesis within particular socio-cultural, political and economic context.

McLuhan and Power's (1989) Tetradic Metaphor

Modern thinking is characterised by left-hemisphere thinking. Ideally and heuristically it is based on the following assumptions:

- Social and natural reality can be understood in terms of quantitative variables, which are sequential; and if controlled through experimental designs, cause and effect can be ascertained.
- This is the goal of scientific study, "to predict and control".
- To sum up: it is "closed, controlled, linear and static"

(McLuhan and Powers, 1989:130) and is further characterised as leading to "squared off, controlled and cultivated environments" (McLuhan and Powers, 1989:134). They conclude that 'either or thinking' leaves no room for alternatives (McLuhan and Powers, 1989:ix). This sort of thinking has come to typify modern, western instrumental thinking.

Traditional thinking is characterised by right-hemisphere thinking. It is based on the following assumptions:

- "Variables are simultaneous and holistic"; if studied we can ascertain 'pattern-like qualities'. . .This is qualitative thinking".
- It is characterised by "both and thinking"; participation is encouraged and enhances thinking; it rejects hierarchy.
- In so far as this thinking emphasises harmony it is also argued to be more feminine. The goal is to establish meaning by listening to the other (McLuhan and Powers, 1989:ix).

Their argument is somewhat stereotypical, however because although some Oriental, African, American or Australian Aboriginals may have had many elements of this thinking in traditional culture, it is dangerous to assume that these characteristics of 'traditional culture' exist in a hermetically sealed form today or in the past. Often the static nature of culture is emphasised for a host of poltical reasons: opposition and survival being just two. It is also dangerous to assume that these ideal-type norms previously created a utopian society. Many traditional societies in the past and today are riven by tyranny, conflict and oppression. We need to recognize the positive and negative potential in all cultures and realize their dynamic permeability.

Inclusive thinking can be facilitated by means of a tetrad based on a metaphor derived from communication research, which can be applied to understanding the role of technology in a postmodern era. The role and function of technology is analysed by means of the tetrad. This analytical tool is useful because it teaches people to look not only at the dark figure in the foreground, but also at the white space in the background. It encourages an ability to think not so much in terms of binary oppositions of right and wrong, black and white, but in terms of paradoxes. Whatever "enhances" society in some way may have some "reversal" impact. Whatever is "retrieved" from previous eras may render current applications obsolete.

The tetrad is a conceptual diagram. It comprises a series of interlinked loops that cover four quadrants, namely: enhancement, retrieval, reversal and obsolescence. The diagram illustrates the interconnections of ideas, events and technology. It highlights the paradox that advances in some areas can lead to retreats in others. Each quadrant is linked with the other. For example: A technological invention introduced within a specific context—without thinking about the ramifications socially, culturally, politically, and economically—can bring about unintended consequences. History has provided many examples of the ways in which the environment and the social fabric have been destroyed as a result of concentrating only on a single quadrant, not the whole picture.

This conceptual thinking tool can help teach us to focus on both the foreground and background, and not just a limited quadrant. By focusing only on what we perceive in the foreground, or figure, we limit our understanding of what is happening in the background.

The 1986 Ottawa Health Charter is the basis for a new approach to development. The links between health and socioeconomic and political development have been underlined by means of the charter, which laid the foundation for a Healthy City approach to development based on a multidisciplinary and intersectoral approach (Davies and Kelly, 1993). The integration across disciplines and sectors is recognised as the basis for bringing about change. The modernist solution to development was to attempt to find answers that would provide a blueprint for socio-engineering to provide "the solution". Modern thinking is patriarchal and bureaucratic, particularly when associated with capitalism (Hettne, 1995). Similarly, it is bureaucratic when it is associated with socialist principles. In both cases, the thinking is technocratic with little emphasis on harmonious respect for nature. Modernist research is positivist in nature, with a view to ascertaining causes and effects on the basis of a representative sample that could be widely generalised to other contexts. Postmodernist thinking is reflexive, contextual and open to the idea that there is no one solution for all situations; it is less bound to structuralist thinking limited to disciplines and single sectors.

As mentioned above, postmodernism can also be nihilistic; so new thinking has to co-create new shared models from the liberative potential of previous models. A sense of connectedness with one's environment learned from indigenous peoples is central to this new thinking and has been rediscovered and given formal recognition through new environmental awareness and pragmatism. "Sustainability," said the Brundtland Report, is a development "that meets the needs of the present without compromising the ability of future generations to meet their own needs" (World Commission, 1987:43, cited in Friedman, 1992:124). The notion of caretaking the environment for future generations is understood in an existential sense by Aboriginal Australians. Their notion of harmonious interplay between people and nature is a form of knowledge that will have to be given more attention if we wish to survive together as global citizens of this planet.

McLuhan and Powers (1989) have applied their tetradic thinking tool to seeing the pluses and minuses and paradoxes associated with the development of networks and communication technology. They have shown by means of this thinking tool that progress has in some respects undermined aspects of human life. The tetrad demonstrates how progress can retrieve and obsolesce some human relations simultaneously. For instance, the global village of communication unites human beings in some senses but alienates, at the same time, because people rationalise not having the same sense of responsibility for all those within their so-called global village.

Flat images, whether in the printed or electronic media, are not seen as real flesh and blood. Instead they become part of a news drama on a par with other television drama and a sense of social distance is the result. In this way our sense of global citizenship rights and responsibilities remains stunted, because news reportage does not cover the human angle in all its pathos and paradox.

De Bono's Thinking Hats

The use of De Bono's six thinking hats is a simple and powerful tool for "thinking about thinking". This helps to empower citizens by expanding their individual human maps and thereby increasing their problem-solving ability. The thinking hat analogy encompasses the elements of information, feelings, addressing the negative and the positive points creatively. If we realise that our thinking is influenced by the sort of hats we and other stakeholders could be wearing, it is a useful introduction to reflexive thinking. We can shift away from thinking simplistically, or within a particular framework, or only looking at the figure and not the background. The thinking hats method can be usefully applied in many contexts, from mediation and conflict resolution to strategic planning and problem-solving. De Bono's "six thinking hats" illustrate six factors that shape our thinking. To extract from and summarise McCann (1992:32):

> White hat: The knowledge hat; the necessary data; the information needed. What's available? The information? Its nature? What's needed? What's missing?, Red hat: The Feelings hat; intuition/ hunches/notions... Feelings always come into it, we just disguise them as logic!; Black hat: The cautious hat, judging the 'fit' of the facts, experience, system, law, policy, ethics; Yellow hat: look at benefits, value, feasibility. Implies sustained effort; Green hat: the creative hat; speculative; new ideas, further alternatives. Is the original hypothesis sustainable? What alternatives? Provocations? This hat creates space for concerted creative thinking; Blue hat: Overview/process control. The metacognitive hat...

The concept is also useful for the purpose of shifting thinking within the confines of a particular framework or map to thinking about choice of framework or, better, to find ways of interpolating across frameworks and its implications for both theory and practice.

Mental "Walk-Throughs" Using Scenarios Help Us Understand the Implications of Assumptions for Research and Practice

Philosophers who specialise in ethics talk about testing out actions in one's mind by thinking whether one would like to be at the receiving end of a particular action and the wider implications of an action. The mental walk-through idea is similar, except that if one uses scenarios, one can obtain input from a number of participants who can weigh up the consequences of particular courses of action. It can be helpful to use mental walk-throughs (Denzin and Lincoln, 1994) to consider the implications of particular sets of assumptions for: 1) definitions of so-called social problems; and 2) the resultant policy and practice. This can stimulate reflexive thinking.

For example, at the request of a government department, a mediation was undertaken between young adolescents who had threatened one another with violence at a school in a small agricultural town in provincial Australia. Australian-born students and Kurdish immigrants, most of whom spoke very little or no English, were unable to communicate with one another. Racism resulted from mistrust and a sense of being unable to cope with the others' difference. This was expressed as follows: "I don't know what he is thinking." "How can we be friends when we don't know what they are thinking?"

Cut backs in welfare policy and the consequent decisions to cut specific language tuition led to new immigrants and refugees being unable to communicate at school. The crux of the issue was that these 12-to-16-year-old boys simply could not express themselves verbally. So physical threats made by gesturing and fights were used as a way of defusing tension.

With the assistance of a skilled Kurdish translator (a highly respected male medical doctor known to the local Kurdish community) the mediation explored the language difficulties with students, parents and teachers. Small discussion groups with boys, teachers and then parents were held in succession at the school and in the homes of the boys for two days. As a result of the initial discussions, a concerned headmaster stressed his commitment to lobby for more language tuition and to celebrate the value of multi-culturalism in the school. Thus some of the causes of the problems were highlighted.

The boys responded well to the introduction of scenarios using thinking hats to consider the problem of their inability to communicate. They were able to see the full range of issues as their perspective widened. Positive and negative emotions, plus a sense of the creative potential and the systemic causes for their shared problems, became clearer to the students. The social, political and economic systems leading to the issue of being unable to communicate proved to be interesting. Histories of arrival, competition for resources, and hopes and fears were shared around the notion of citizenship rights and responsibilities. The time of the school conflict coincided with media reports about the Australian political party, One Nation, led by Pauline Hanson. The Australian students were aware of the content of this coverage. At that time, Hanson spoke strongly about the impact of global markets on rural Australians and provincial towns, with a strongly racist tone directed at the way in which "Immigrants and Aboriginals(sic) benefited at the cost of others". In times of economic scarcity, competitive, adversarial thinking tends to be revived by Right Wing groups. Problems are "solved" by scapegoating. The power play of win or lose has repeated itself again and again throughout history.

The categories right/wrong, insider/outsider were used by the Australian students and their parents at the outset of the mediation. Right from the beginning both groups of children and their parents were receptive to problem-solving through mediation and dialogue, because they feared the consequences of violence. This fear was also fuelled by media stories of recent massacres in American schools committed by children using semi-automatic or assault rifles. Simultaneously, the media also covered the farmers and gun enthusiasts lobbying against the Australian government decision to ban semi-automatic weapons. The media stories were discussed and both parents and children felt that they needed to "nip the problem in the bud". Kurdish parents said they would do everything in their power to ensure that their children "kept out of trouble" and concentrated on their schooling. They were fearful, though, that the discrimination from which they had fled would dog them and that their children's lives would not improve. The Australian parents said they, too, would ensure that their children did not land up in trouble, but they were fearful about the standard of education at school because of the obviously inadequate resources.

To help with language training, the school principal agreed to put in place practical supports that would not jeopardise the chances of other students. It was acknowledged that the problems could not be solved through changing styles of thinking without providing the much-needed English language training to help facilitate the integration of young Kurds.

The boys role-played a fairly low-key scenario, giving and receiving abuse and mistrust. They were asked to use a particular style of behaviour: aggressive, submissive, cunning and insincere, wise and understanding. After the role-play, they were asked to describe how they felt. Each boy had a turn at feeling the victim. The Kurdish medical doctor at this point led a discussion on what it is to be a strong man in Australian society; how being wise and turning one's back on provocation is quite acceptable, if one makes an effort to ensure that the issue is addressed by the school and not by one's peers, or worse, elder brothers.

To help with a discussion of citizenship and the struggles that some people have for minimal rights, a video of young people in South Africa talking about their hopes introduced the notion of life chances and cultural perceptions. The roles played by socio, political and economic systems beyond the classroom were discussed.

The mediation helped young people to reconsider their rights and responsibilities. The way in which this session was conducted aimed at shifting thinking needs to be contrasted with the recent notion of 'straight talk' programs used by departments of correctional services in the United States and United Kingdom, and currently being piloted in Australia for young people considered to be 'at risk' of committing crimes. These programs aim to change thinking through tough, straight talking. In some cases the programs are behaviourist in orientation and focus on warning young people about the consequences of specific types of behaviour labelled 'at risk'. Graphic slides are shown of the consequences of crime; namely, a prison sentence accompanied by life stories of ex-offenders or current offenders who wish young people to benefit from their experience. Whilst the motivation of many of the offenders is sincere, the social context of their behaviour needs to be explored through discussion with young people. Communication for education needs to be "open" not "top down," if creative learning is to occur (McIntyre, 1996). Young people need to be active participants in the discussions, not merely passive listeners to dramatic life stories that do not necessarily explore why and how lives changed. Nor do these stories explore what constitutes social justice, or the rights and responsibilities of citizens to one another. Participants need an understanding of the way in which competitive thinking limits our ability to solve problems.

Lateral Thinking and Inclusive "Both and Logic" Rather Than "Either or Logic"

De Bono's 1993 book, *Water Logic: The Alternative to I am Right and You Are Wrong,* outlines a tool for encouraging us to map out perceptions so that we can understand one another by using pictures to aid abstract thinking. This is a very useful way to help people explore diversity.

This is the first step to help us move away from simple deduction and induction. Deduction—as any introductory logic text such as Salmon's *Logic Foundations of Philosophy* (1973) will explain—makes explicit what is implicit in the premises of an argument; whereas induction goes beyond what is implicit in the basic premises and makes generalisations beyond the premises. Thinking laterally and reflexively helps us to move away from linear social planning approaches, and to think laterally to consider the various participants and stakeholders' perceptions. Organic thinking based on what De Bono calls 'water logic' assists us to make organic representations of thinking such as spidergrams which help us to represent and elaborate the complexity of ideas rather than simplifying them. Organic representations of conceptual thinking (Tyson, 1989) such as spidergrams represent complex ideas and perceptions. The "body of the spider" can represent a summary of central assumptions and "the legs " can represent derived ideas. De Bono's conceptual maps of the shape of people's constructs of a situation comprise simple circles and lines to map out the flow points and connections. Techniques such as these help us to avoid narrow dogma of I am right and you are wrong or the notion of thinking in terms of simplistic binary oppositions (Levy- Strauss, 1987).

This is a useful tool for *conflict resolution, needs assessment and evaluation* because it can be used to describe in careful detail the point of view of "the other"and the way in which their ideas fit together. In other words, it helps the listener to gain a sense of the personal logic of the other. Tools such as these provide an aid to active listening in an attempt to understand the way "the other" thinks. Connectedness and lateral thinking can better serve social justice. The approach is not nihilistic and is rooted in the process of interpersonal sharing to find the best approximate truth.

4

Ecological and Critical Humanism (Eco-Humanism): Creating Webs of Meaning Through Paradigm Dialogue

What are shared webs of meaning and why should we try to create them? The notion that intellectual 'expert' knowledge is the preserve of those with secondary and tertiary education has been challenged by writers such as Gramsci, Paulo Freire, Polanyi, Orlando Fals-Borda, and Robert Chambers (Fals-Borda and Rahman, 1991:127). The 'lived experiences' and 'personal knowledge' of people who are so-called 'poor,' 'uneducated' in a formal sense and in need of 'development' by so-called 'experts' from 'educated' sectors of societies has been called into question. If we can learn from 'the other' and establish two-way learning then we can start to create shared meanings.

Creating webs of meaning is the goal of a re-defined global citizenship for a sustainable social justice. To achieve this we need to find interpolations across barriers that keep us apart. This process is about finding the contours that link the different parts of the human cosmological map in order to forge **global human knowledge**. The Popperian notion of falsifiication is the cornerstone of Western science and although it was used as the justification for the worst forms of empiricism, it can also unlock the doors of Western science to global wisdom. By this I mean that if taken-for-granted ideas are subjected to falsification attempts against other processes and **frames of know-**

ing, then our respective notions of reality and notions of how we obtain knowledge could be enhanced. Quite possibly the areas of overlap could lead to new insights and understanding in the world.

It is only by forging webs of meaning across the divides of culture and economics that we can end sectarian violence and the philosophy that "the market dictates" the extent to which we can behave in ethical ways towards one another, and the extent to which we are willing to consider the fragility of our environment (see chapter 5 for further discussion). 'Paradigm dialogue' is a reflexive stance that nevertheless has some normative assumptions underpinning it, namely:

—The closest we can get to a sense of "truth" is through openness and dialogue. EcoHumanism (EH) embraces the liberative potential of the notion that science attempts to test the probability of "truth" through attempts at falsification, not verification. It differs in so far as it assumes truth to be iterative, rather than objective—except for the ultimate truth, namely our shared ecosystem and biology. Hence the EH researcher is humble not arrogant. Most importantly this 'ism' abhors 'experts' who think they know better than 'non-experts'. Paradigm dialogue is used to test out the extent to which ideas are ethical by working together with stakeholders to explore the diversity of their thinking in the interests of preserving their common good and domain.

—The macro level of structural shapers is as relevant as the micro level of human creativity and perception; they are (to import a Marxist concept) "part of the same moment". They address the issue of power rooted in technology and expressed as access to capital (both economic -and information-based).

—They strive to find interpolations or common denominators across disciplines and to work against the establishment of barriers. EH takes cognisance of the broad sociological perspectives (humanism, structural functionalism, conflict theory, feminism, critical theory and poststructuralism) and their potential value for helping us to understand social reality. It avoids the nihilism of postmodernism and maintains the optimism of a revised humanism. It strives for "both and thinking". Discourse refers to a system of ideas, and Ecological Humanism (see McIntyre, 1995 on critical humanism, a precursor to this concept) is largely a reflexive stance; it needs to be stressed that it does have some basic normative assumptions underpinning it.

—EH has a holistic approach to understanding causation and acknowledges that technological thinking should not exploit nature but strive for sustainable development in harmony with nature. We may have "removed the copyright of life from God" (Castells, 1996:48) "but we are a long way off knowing how to sustain life though understanding the links across technology, humanity and the environment".

—"Personal troubles" need to be understood in terms of "public issues" (to use C. Wright Mills 1975 concept), but the personal responsibility for change should never be abrogated for mere structural explanations.

A belief in the universal human spirit guides the creation of theory and practice in harmony with people and nature. Spiritual health and well-being—in the sense described by First Nations of "being human through other people" and through harmony with the environment—is the goal, not merely "changing the balance of power" through narrowly political strategies. Humility is a theme being rediscovered by Western thinkers who are no longer sure that they have all the answers. EH does not pretend to be a new panacea, but merely to assist in developing theoretical and methodological literacy.

Gouldner's (1971) term can be drawn out contextually by stakeholders who apply this tool. Postmodernism is liberative if it doesn't lapse into throwing out the potential of *human rational* thought embedded in science *at its best*, along with the *arrogant instrumentalism* of science *at its worst*. If we allow the extremes of social relativism that simply aim to understand human constructs and refuse to value them in terms of a shared human reality, we open the floodgates of chaos and nihilism. Poststructuralism is liberative if it allows us to understand that human beings are not entirely regimented by structures and that they have creative potential, as long as we do not believe that structures do not have a role shaping life chances. The potential for nihilism exists in this strand if social neglect occurs.

According to Barry Jones (1990), politicians need to be able to hold more than one big idea in their minds at the same time. Alvin Gouldner wrote in his book in the 1970s about " the coming crisis in western sociology", concerning the need to think in terms of "the liberative potential" of theories not merely in terms of competing paradigms. MIT economist Lester Thurow (1996) has stressed that economic models are bereft of original thought because the orthodoxy of economic rationalism remains largely unchallenged by mainstream economists. The likes of economists such as Krugman (1994), Hugh Stretton (1990) and Argyrous and Stillwell (1996) need to be listened to simply because debate that leads to interpolations of ideas (Flood and Romm, 1996) is essential for creative problem-solving.

The logical links across assumptions and values that underpin theories, methodologies and methods can be carefully mapped out so that we can understand the implications of our values and assumptions for practice.

Thinking about thinking does not try to develop a grand theory but merely to develop a realisation that a balance between diversity and commonality is essential for the survival of the ecosystem. This ultimate wisdom is summed up by the yin/yang Taoist symbol.

EH came about as a result of: 1) reflection on Western, Asian and African religions; 2) personal experiences whilst working within a range of cultures; 3) reading critical theorists such as Giddens, Gouldner and Habermas; and 4) feminist writers such as Fonow and Cook, 1991; Stanley and Wise 1993; and Bell 1983. These writers understand connections between patriarchal and matriarchal family structures in a range of economic contexts and the life chances of women. So much feminist writing has been for and about women in Western capitalist societies. It is important to learn from a range of non-Western feminisms.

EH is also informed by a range of methodological approaches which have attempted to understand the voice of the other (see Fine in Denzin and Lincoln, 1994), the person who is researched and represented or misrepresented by the researcher. The power imbalance in this relationship needs to be addressed. An EH approach explores boundaries and overlaps amongst people, in order to address power imbalances and to attempt to restore harmony within and amongst people and their environment. The links between health and development in terms of physical, mental and spiritual well-being have received increased recognition in recent years as a result of the official ratification of the World Health Organisation. These links have long been understood in societies where debased forms of positivist science have not channelled thinking into rigid compartments. EH cannot be categorised as postmodernist, because it is normative in some respects; it is poststructuralist and aims to be both transcultural and transcategorical. EH is rooted in an awareness of the paradoxical nature of reality and the need to achieve harmony and balance amongst opposites.

"Either or", binary oppositional thinking is a product of simplistic versions of Aristotelian thinking that categorises material into boxes. Rather than trying to prove 'the other' wrong through dialogue, we need styles of thinking that find common denominators through dialogue, which establishes the links across areas of knowledge and identifies the areas of difference. Identity politics at its worst is expressed in racism, nationalism, sexism and other forms of sectarianism and bigotry. It could be addressed by focusing on the reasons for fear or a sense of scarcity and providing space for some differences, which are essential for cultural creativity whilst emphasising and reassuring one another of common needs and common goals.

Inclusive thinking tracing common webs of meaning can be taught through thinking tools. Teaching is a vital arena for social transformation and the role of educational institutions at all levels is to teach people to work with ideas rather than within the boundaries of prescribed orthodoxies. Thurow (1996) ends his book by saying that Columbus succeeded in finding a new world not because he was lucky, but because he was prepared to set sail in a new direction despite resistance from those around him. A belief in individual human creativity and innovative thinking needs to be tempered by an understanding that we are part of a delicate ecological system in which we are caretakers.

Theoretical literacy is a response to a postmodernist reality of competing constructs of 'truth'. Transcultural tools help us avoid thinking in terms of specific cultural categories 'boxed in' by barriers. This is the conceptual image evoked when we talk of 'cross-cultural' thinking. Instead, transcultural perception is about attempting to see beyond the narrow categories of one set of cultural lenses and view the common denominators which underpining our humanity.

Thinking tools comprise analytical concepts that organise, pattern and question thoughts about the social and natural world. Introducing concepts of global citizenship and human rights and responsibility, social movements and transcultural webs of meaning in a specific ontological and epistemological sense open up some new dimensions in thinking. Each theoretical concept is meaningless unless it is explained in terms of the assumptions and values on which it is based. The way we understand or interpret the world also shapes the way in which we research it, the way we practice, and the way we make policy—not to mention the content of the policy. So the definition one social theorist, journalist or government policy-maker gives to a concept could differ dramatically from the next writer, thinker, or practitioner, depending on a host of factors ranging from personal life experience and political values to mental well being that morning!

The evolution of the concept Ecological Humanism is explained because it gives the social contexts in which the thesis is developed. Previously Ragg (1977) stressed the need to consider "people not cases". Drawing on philosophy and social work theory and practice, Ragg concludes with the exhortation that social workers should not be merely humanistic but also critical. He coined the term "critical humanism".

In *Achieving Social rights and Responsibility: Towards a Critical Humanist Approach to Community Development* (1995), I tried to develop Critical Humanism (CH) from a different disciplinary base—namely social anthropology, sociology and Participatory Action Research (PAR) in community development. A version of Critical Humanism (McIntyre, 1995 and 1996) came about as a result of responding to the humanistic ideas of Norma Romm, when she headed a theory group at the University of South Africa. By 1992 Romm and Veronica Mckay collaborated on *People's Education in Theoretical Perspective: Towards the Development of a Critical Humanist Approach* which I read in 1997, once Romm had read the manuscripts I sent to her. Their book evolved in the context of their work in education and the development of theory for the South African context.

My version of CH (the precursor of EH) came about as a result of personal experiences as an action researcher in a range of urban and rural contexts, and as a university and community teacher. The ideas that led to this book were honed whilst I was a lecturer at the Salisbury Campus of the University of South Australia—closed as a result of cost-cutting. The campus was situated in an area described in the Social Health Atlas of South Australia (South Australian Health Commission, 1990) as having the highest rates of unemployment, and scoring low in terms of most of the socio-economic indicators. The campus provided a beacon of opportunity for adults and recent school-leavers. Immigrants, single-parent families and Aboriginal people predominated in the area, and community development was a popular subject choice.

The tension between the structural thinkers' desire to understand the shapers of life chances and the humanists' desire to represent the perceptions and voice of the individual is misplaced. Understanding the implications of both positions on ontological and epistemological maps would help make academics and practitioners realise that both halves of the map can help to make up the whole picture. Sets of assumptions underpinning theoretical positions need to be critically unpacked so that the implications for practice are understood.

"Archaeologically" the community health work of Jackson et al. (1989) in Melbourne, whom I draw on (1995), links the ideas in some respects to Ragg, but I develop the notions of theoretical and methodological literacy. More recently Ife (1996) develops the themes of Critical Humanism in relation to social work. Whereas Ragg ends his work with an exhortation concerning the understanding of people within their social contexts, not as mere cases, I attempt to develop a theoretical and methodological praxis that would enable people to step outside the constraints of particular paradigms. Ecological Humanism, however, builds in a specifically environmental focus, and places faith not merely in the potential of people to bring about change but underlines the way in which people and nature are systemically linked.

As far as their understanding of social stratification is concerned EH thinkers believe that people can challenge social structures that support the interests of the 'haves'. No matter how great the risks, individuals and groups of people have lobbied for changes through the centuries. EH thinkers, for example, choose neither socialism nor capitalism as "the answer". They are always interested in confronting the "bad news" (Romm, 1986) of an approach. It is understood that truth lies in the preparedness to listen to the viewpoint of others, whilst keeping a grasp on the key assumption of individual potential and creativity, and the common values of human rights and dignity. Social justice solutions are always an interim best fit for a specific time and place and in order to meet the common interests of groups of people within their ecosystems. Individuals and groups should be encouraged to be debunkers of taken-for-granted solutions.

EH avoids becoming rooted at the micro level of people's subjective experience and neglecting the relevance of social structures in shaping experiences. Social structures do pose challenges and provide obstacles but if people believe in their creative ability—as demonstrated through the ages—they will have hope and optimism for the future. They will believe that they can continue to adjust the balance of power in order to ensure that democracy is enhanced rather than eroded. Our goal as global citizens is to facilitate social action based on a sense of shared responsibility. This could help to develop a more democratic society. EH draws on Critical Theory and is gender sensitive. The liberative potential of humanism and poststructuralism are formative aspects. EH cannot be categorised as postmodernist, because it is normative in some respects; it aims to be both transcultural and transcategorical. The approach is rooted in an awareness of the paradoxical nature of reality and the need to achieve harmony and balance amongst opposites. In this respect it draws on Taoism.

There are many discourses within feminism. The sets of assumptions have perhaps only one common denominator, namely a belief that women's experiences are different from men's experiences. The reasons for these differences are disputed amongst feminists. Those with a socialist orientation attribute the differences to a combination of capitalism and patriarchy; those with a radical orientation analyse the different life chances and experiences in terms of the limitations placed on women living within patriarchal structures. Some radical feminists are militant; others, such as those with a liberal orientation, believe in trying to achieve integration based on shared interests—whether they are economic or cultural. Some socialist feminists believe that class and cultural position undermine any possibility of a shared feminist paradigm!

Some African, Australian Aboriginal and American Indian feminists argue that traditional matriarchal systems provide parallel rights and protect women's interests. Wolf (1993) points out that women are able to use power to achieve their goals; However, not all women have the vote and cannot therefore use power groupings to change the status quo. She forgets that not all women are middle-class Americans. She generalises their life experience to all women, without emphasis on the very different life chances and life experiences of women in other socio-cultural, economic and political circumstances.

If we look at women's statistics (United Nations, 1991), we see that women do not outnumber men everywhere as she suggests, because of the practice of infanticide on female babies in some contexts! Wolf's suggestions are pertinent in contexts where women have already achieved a measure of power. Also her distinction between 'victim feminism' and 'power feminism' poses feminism in binary oppositional logic. There is a role for both and many other types as well. Aboriginal women are subject to domestic violence and tend to avoid "dobbing in their men" to the police because they understand that Aboriginal men share their social position and their futures are linked. They also understand that they play the role of absorbing the anger of marginalised men whose frustration boils over at home when topped up by alcohol[5]. Her point about not looking backward once one has gained a measure of power—and lapsing into victim mode—is well taken, however, provided we read her statements as applying first and foremost to women living in developed Western nations. In other contexts, survival in terms of meeting basic social needs can focus women's energy in different ways. The problems of "either or thinking" continue to permeate innovative theories.

Tensions between feminism and humanism exist, but EH reflects on the continuities and overlaps amongst these positions. It attempts to draw out from feminism the 'liberative potential' concerned with equal rights and is sensitive to the range of categories, in addition to gender that can lead to discrimination. Patriarchy and capitalism are considered to be equally important shapers of the life chances of women. The dramatic changes in family structure in most parts of the Western developed world have come about largely as a result of changes in contraceptive technology. As women's options widen, they obtain more education, employment opportunities and wealth. It cannot be denied that women continue to have less power and fewer resources in most parts of the world, but their potential social roles have expanded beyond the patriarchal family.

This has led to reevaluations of gender and sexuality by men and women. An increasing recognition of the social nature of gender roles and the biological continuum between male and female sexuality becomes possible when there is a shift away from thinking in terms of biological binary oppositions. The debate about the rights of homosexuals and transsexuals would become less fraught if human cultural thinking emphasised the liberative potential of systemic thinking. Cultural acceptance of specific roles for homo sapiens is closely linked with survival strategies. Sexuality and gender roles that limit the number of births make sense because they make possible the highest quality of life for the optimum number of people (Colinvaux, 1980) until further environments can be colonised.

How does EH avoid the problem of denying the particular experience of women? The answer is that it explores commonalties and diversity that exist as a result of age, gender, level of ability, class, culture, race and religion, for instance. The paradoxical nature of many social issues is not brushed aside by EH. It is explored. Paradigm dialogue for systemic thinking could be regarded as a bridge across strands of humanism and feminism.

Fonow and Cook (1991) and Stanley and Wise (1993) discuss the key themes in feminist research. They see feminist research as advocacy research that gives a voice to women. They emphasise the value of combining qualitative and quantitative methods. They echo the themes addressed in the works of Freire, Polanyi and other critical theorists who have used ethnography to empower rather than merely record the meanings of informants.

The distortions of the world of informants compared to those of the male point of view are pointed out; however, the contributions of female anthropologists are not highlighted. The ontological and epistemological ideas mentioned in these books are not entirely new. The roots of EH are linked with strands of social anthropology, that stressed the point of view of the insider living within a particular social, political and economic context. The work of Marxists who critiqued social structures also influences this notion of deconstruction, which is really just a sophisticated term for 'unpacking', 'debunking' or asking critical questions. The role of reflexivity in research is important because it allows for ongoing self-monitoring and monitoring what the research results mean to the various parties, rather than merely checking out reliability and validity in the strictly positivist sense in which they are used. I use the latter terms in a loose sense. Denzin and Lincoln (1994) and Ian Dey (1993) argue that number and meaning are closely linked in defining constructs, rather than in the more literal descriptive sense in which Miles and Huberman (1984) use the concepts.

EH is unashamedly instrumentalist, in so far as it provides a framework for theoretical thinking framing action that responds to the needs of people who are marginalised through understanding stakeholders' perceptions. It is substantivist, insofar as all analysis and implementation occurs in a particular context, and it is normative, insofar as working with all of the stakeholders to find a workable nonviolent solution.

Whilst feminists have driven nonobjective approaches they are not solely responsible for claiming new paradigms. Also not responsible is Peter Reason (1988) who wrote *Human Inquiry in Action* in which he outlined a so-called 'new paradigm'. Guba and Lincoln (1989) who wrote *Fourth Generation Evaluation* which outlines the principles of a constructivist approach and Denzin and Lincoln (1994), who detail a host of qualitative research methodologies, demonstrate the wide range of sources to which their thinking is linked. The cultural divide between some so-called mainstream thinking and feminist works is beginning to close. The notion of reflection or reflexivity is evident in the humanist work of, for example Mead (1974), Berger (1976, 1977) and in the critical work of Habermas (1974) or Foucault (1980). So the notion of reflexivity that existentialist thinkers such as Sartre introduced has also had an influence. Reflexivity is essential in order to avoid sectarian thinking.

Feminist thinking is, however, unique in its explicit highlighting and acknowledgement of the emotional content and feelings of the research participants. There is no pretence at neutrality, instead emotions are discussed openly and an attempt is made to reflect on the implications of emotional content for their research, instead of pretending that emotions do not exist (Stanley and Wise, 1993, Fonow and Cook, 1991). There are of course both positive and negative aspects to this contribution. Emotion is recognised as being part of the research process and is not " bracketed out". This contributes to a greater sense of the connections between the researcher and research subject(s).

If we understand humanism as recognition of rights—irrespective of gender, race and socio-cultural categories—in other words, if human diversity is celebrated, then EH can be regarded as an essential thinking tool for bridging theories based on sectarian understanding. Johnson (1994) has argued along parallel lines for a radical re-thinking of humanism and feminism. In this work, however, citizenship has been linked with a critical humanism based on a respect for diversity and for the essential common denominators that link all humankind, namely one biosphere. As global citizens, we need to forge webs of transcultural meanings if we are to achieve any form of social justice locally and internationally. The two common denominators *of shared bodily needs* and *one environment* need to be expressed in transcultural forms that recognise diversity and freedom to the extent they it allow for the future survival of all.

Ontological and epistemological maps give the reader a sense of how the so-called "paradigms of knowledge" can be seen instead as "constructs of knowledge" and that these constructs can be mapped, using lines to symbolise the contour links across the positions. We can interpolate across positions and create new constructs that are not 'boxed' in discrete ways but that instead have some 'core and overlapping' ideas. By seeing connections rather than barriers across constructs, we can develop clusters of ideas and themes that inform and educate one another. Reading paradigms as constructs can help us weave new meanings.

Because the central tenet of EH is that the closest we can get to truth is through interpersonal sharing of ideas and reflection on these ideas, it enables a liberation from doctrinaire, blueprint positions or ideology. This is done without lapsing into the potentially nihilistic trap of postmodernism, which can undermine the notion of common rights and responsibility—by virtue of our shared humanity. EH is not postmodernist in that it does not eschew all notions of truth and is underpinned by assumptions that shape practice. The thinking of Habermas who emphasised the goal of achieving "nonviolent intersubjectivity" as a goal for democracy and the creative potential of people (Beilharz, 1993:133) is just one of the influential approaches shaping EH that strives to provide some specific action principles for social movements. Another crucial contribution made by Habermas, according to Bjorn Hettne (1995) who cites Bernstein (1985), is that he continues to emphasise the relevance of rationalism rather than extreme forms of relativism. In other words, he warns against the nihilism of postmodernism. Noam Chomsky (1993:286) makes a more recent and passionate plea as follows:

> . . . their left counterparts today often seek to deprive working people of these tools of emancipation [social movements and the press, author's addition], informing us that the 'project of the Enlightenment' is dead, that we must abandon the 'illusions' of science and rationality, a message that will gladden the hearts of the powerful, delighted to monopolise these instruments for their own use. . .

In a fast-changing global context we are no longer able to deny diversity. We are confronted each day by a range of assumptions and values. The way we make sense of them shapes our decisions. Do we attempt to fit all the new input into the old paradigm with which we are familiar or do we simply discard them in a Kuhnian (1970) sense when we find anomalies, without trying to find some grounds for extracting the liberative potential of each? Global knowledge can only be developed through respect for diversity and common denominators. For instance, Flood and Romm (1996) summarise the range of approaches called action learning, action science, participatory action research and collaborative research. They exhort an interpolation of approaches that strive to give power to 'the other', rather than achieve power *over* the other in terms of research, practice and policy outcomes.

Tools from the above mentioned thinkers have helped shape my version of EH—a praxis tool which does not pretend to be a new panacea, but strives to develop theoretical and methodological literacy. The liberative potential of theories can be drawn out contextually by stakeholders who apply this tool. The logical links across the assumptions and values that underpin theories, methodologies and methods can be carefully mapped out to help stakeholders understand the implications of their values and assumptions for practice.

5

The Rights and Responsibilities of Global Citizens: Pragmatism, Ethics, and Survival at the Coalface of Bureaucracies

> A reworked critical theory, such as I conceive of it at any rate, would mix utopianism and realism in equal measure (Giddens, 1995:xix).

Bureaucracies have been the organisational forms used by mechanised industrialised societies with associated management styles and regulations. Networks and matrices will be the organisational forms used by networked societies with management styles that either maximise fluidity at the expense of democracy or use fluidity to enhance creativity. **Logically ethical practice will increase, as the value of systemic, cooperative thinking becomes apparent to all.** The use of computers has enabled creative thinkers to delegate the basic categorisation of knowledge to computers that work on basic binary oppositional logic. It is now possible to use the information in a multiplicity of ways in order to solve problems. This frees problem-solvers from thinking in terms of narrow categories and hierarchies or even in terms of one meta-theory. Information literacy is no longer restricted to a few categories, but is opened to follow weblike routes through data to create specific contextual responses to diversity. Exceptions to the bureaucratic rule become increasingly possible and the ontological responsibility to tap this diversity—whilst preserving the one truth, namely our sharedness in terms of biology and ecology becomes an ethical imperative.

Survival in all sectors will depend on the ability of people to tap into the new information networks. The notion of splits between the private and public sector are becoming increasingly blurred and if democratic and ecological rights are to be maintained, regained or gained, an ability to use political, social and economic networking will be essential. Participatory Action Research (PAR) helps to re-work categories through communication based on listening and helping to re-frame paradigms into new webs of shared meaning.

A History of Management Used in Bureaucracies

The traditional Taylorist model is based on scientific management principles and the assumption that by nature people are lazy. According to these principles, the responsibility of the employer is to control workers' time and motion scientifically and to pay their wages. In line with fragmented, categorical thinking associated with scientific management at its worst, little attention was paid to working conditions or the personal needs of workers. Changes were introduced by psychologist Lilian Gilbreth public scientist and Mary Parker Follett in the late 1920s (Fox and Urwick, 1973, Wolf, 1989; and Graham, 1991) Later in the 1930s Elton Mayo (1945), a social anthropologist whose discipline tends to be more holistic and qualitative initiated participatory styles of management and assumed that people work better when they are fulfilled through their work. Gradually, a shift in emphasis occurred away from task relationships to include socio-emotional aspects of human relations. Management theory began to take into account that participation of workers in decision-making was not only motivating and good for production levels, but also good for management. Workers 'personal knowledge' (Polanyi, 1962) could help enhance creative thinking and reduce risks.

The philosophy of participatory management is humanistic and premised on a belief in people's creative potential and a desire to fulfill higher-order needs on Maslow's (1954) hierarchy, such as self-esteem and self-actualisation, not merely lower-order maintenance needs (Herzberg, 1975). The early forms of participatory management developed in response to the ill effects of top-down management. Similarly, as far as leadership studies are concerned, there has been a shift away from looking merely at the leaders and their associated characteristics to include a study of the interactive group processes of leading. Researchers such as Fiedler, Hersey and Blanchard, Vroom and Yetton (Vecchio, 1988) realised that management styles should focus on the potential of workers, not the extent to which they need to be controlled scientifically or made to feel useful; not merely to improve human relations, but because people are the most important resource in work situations (Ouchi in Kaplan and Ziegler, 1985). The 'power with' people approach pioneered by Follett in the United States in the 1930s—whose work Japanese management theorists are well aware of and that contributed to respectful work with people in 'quality circles' in the 70s and 80s (Graham, 1991)—needs to remain at the forefront of management practice and not be set aside as 'fear of global markets' drives managers to revert to 'power over' people rather than integrative approaches. This aspect of Asian management is valuable in contrast to financial management practices that have come about as a result of global capitalism and greed.

The social context of workplace relations has been the focus of the work of Elizabeth Moss Kanter (1989, 1991), a Harvard Business School academic and social anthropologist, who is interested in finding ways to work collaboratively in the business context as a result of her experience working on kibbutzim. By studying networks, we can establish the power relations existing amongst players or stakeholders in business enterprises. If employers and employees are seen first and foremost as global citizens who wish to maximise their chances of long-term survival on the planet, collaboration based on "pooling, allying and linking"—to use Moss-Kanter's (1989) concept—is the order of the day. Problem-solving using nonhierarchical approaches to collaborative problem-solving needs to be developed within schools and places of work, and expanded beyond the workplace to include participatory citizenship across all domains of life.

Participatory-facilitative leadership takes the human resources model further. It is based on seeing workers as citizens with rights, responsibilities and potential, and argues that the workplace is a political environment where people can either be encouraged to make a contribution or made to feel like distrusted, naughty children.

Links can be drawn across positivist thinking styles that emphasise a distinction between subject and object and control of outcomes by experts, management philosophy, and attitudes towards workers. The function of managers in capitalist and socialist production is to control labour in order to extract profit through surplus value, or to provide the means to build industry in the case of socialism. In both contexts, the technological emphasis has been on mechanisation and extraction of surplus value from people and the environment. In a computerised, networked society (Castells, 1996-1998) the domain for profit extraction includes not only the production sphere—where poor workers in the First and Third World continue to be exploited along with their environments—but also profit maximisation through exchange. Knowing how, where and when to sell products and, even more importantly, knowing how to use stock markets to bet on products and services favours the information rich.

In the past, the alienation from the whole process of work and the contradiction between labour and the capitalist class has been softened: firstly, as a result of the setting up of welfare states in most capitalist states; and secondly, by the increased ability of working classes to buy a vast array of consumer goods. The "affluent worker" as conceptualised by Goldthorpe et al. (1968) seems to have little in common with the exploited labouring poor of Marx's era. In the pragmatic 1990s, however, computerisation has led to changes in all aspects of economic life. Pressures to compete in global markets have led to the rise of economic rationalism and, once more, to versions of Taylorism in a context in which the "labouring poor" are becoming increasingly de-unionised. The connections between high unemployment, worsening working conditions and de-unionisation need to be carefully understood by the labouring poor who count themselves "lucky to have a job".

As markets unite, workers and the unemployed find themselves competing with the lumpenproletariat in the poorest sections of the global economy. Capitalist control of the labour process has been extended and enhanced by the growth of modern management, which has reinvented Taylorism with the excuse that even more surplus value has to be extracted in order to be competitive during the downturn in global markets. Added to this exchange value in futures markets has added a further dimension to wealth creation and loss by the "information rich". The crisis in October 1998 of the largest Hedge Funds in the United States has brought home the lesson that betting on the direction of share prices has to factor in human and environmental considerations.

As we move toward the new millennium, welfare-state policies have shifted away from the universal right to welfare toward residualism; as much effort as possible is being directed toward minimising business taxes—often at the expense of private households—to attract investment and maximise profits.

The goals and objectives of traditional generic management have been almost entirely focused on the pursuit of profit through efficiency. The drive for profit-motivated efficiency through top-down, 'power over' forms of communication is precisely what has been identified (Karpin, 1994, cited by Delaney, 1996, in written commentary on this material) as the major barrier to essential change in contemporary generic management. This barrier has polarised and separated workers and employers. Workers lose their dignity as a result of autocratic styles of management; and there is also an opportunity cost to employers—namely the loss of the employee creative potential that could be used to increase output (Denys Delaney, 1996, op. cit.). Empowering managers as well as workers through the application of the principles of EH could be of benefit to all.

Managers who consider their workers as autonomous individuals with basic rights and responsibilities will set the tone for mutual respect and adult behaviour. EH does not deny the potential for conflict or the existence of 'power over' relationships; however, it does strive to address these by respecting the dignity and rights of the individual, while also bearing in mind the broader context of structural challenges.

Ideally, a sense of global citizenship rights and responsibilities could begin in the workplace, if management styles were to foster an understanding of social responsibility through modelling these roles.

The Shifts in Management Styles are Associated with Socio-Economic History

Enhanced productivity is the order of the day. The rules of global markets have raised the spectre of the need for governments to balance their budgets and open up their markets. The welfare state in France, the United States, Canada, Britain, New Zealand and Sweden is undergoing transformation in response to market pressures (Jones, 1992). In economics, the monetarist approach or neo-Liberalism is posed against neo-Keynesianism.

In response, citizens need to link working life and social life with public responsibility, given that social change cannot be achieved in the ballot box, because choices provided by the state do not always help global democracy. As global citizens we have to find other bases for change. One obvious arena is the workplace. Although there is a crisis within traditional workplace relations and management as companies try to respond in a top-down manner to the pressures of global markets, there is an alternative approach.

The notion of ordained or born leaders has been challenged along with the principles on which it is based. According to Johnson and Johnson (1987) one of the positive outflows of group dynamics research was the discovery that in group situations there can be more than one leader. As a result of small-group research on leadership, Bales (1958) found that leadership roles could be filled by different people with "socio-emotional" and "task-oriented characteristics", respectively. His notion of differentiated leadership and Alinsky's (1972) notion of indigenous leadership are liberative in that they recognise the creative potential of all people.

This theme of the creative, responsible individual was also emphasised by management theorists who can be grouped in the so-called human resources school of management. They premised their belief in the individual, even if it was associated with the profit motive and motivation of employees! Follett (Fox and Urwick, 1973 and Graham, 1991) coined the phrase 'power with' not 'power over' in leadership, and Elton Mayo (1945) stressed the need for people to feel in control and appreciated. Hersey and Blanchard (1988) stressed "personal power" as being more important than "position power" for leadership.

Alinsky also believed in leadership not "headship" as a basis for development. The task of a facilitator is to find indigenous representative leaders of various interest groups and work with them to empower them and the people they represent. Within the workplace a sense of global citizenship rights and responsibilities can be fostered.

Tension and stress reduction, as well as increased productivity and worker satisfaction, can be achieved through enhancing employer-employee relations. This can be accomplished by valuing the creative potential of workers, who are seen as citizens with both rights and responsibilities. This is an extended version of the argument put forward by Elton Mayo. He argued that people are most productive when: a) they have the opportunity to express themselves in a creative sense; b) when their contributions are respected in the working environment—based on treating workers as ends in themselves, not merely means to an end. These principles could transform what we mean by participation and facilitation.

But action is also required by citizens concerned with maintaining democratic rights, rather than remaining passive victims of "the law of the market". Which Stretton (1990) stresses this needs to be governed with people in mind because economic laws cannot be relied upon to solve the key challenges of our time: foreign debt, unemployment and poor industrial relations. Furthermore, the challenge of environmental sustainability needs to be factored into all considerations.

Applying an EH approach to workplace empowerment unleashes the potential creativity of both managers and employees. Participatory involvement based on a philosophy of belief in the capacity of people could enhance workplace relations locally and internationally. Thinking tools facilitate better planning with all the stakeholders and could help to address the barriers amongst stakeholders. The conceptual boundaries and overlaps amongst people could be identified to improve project planning and problem-solving with stakeholders from a range of disciplines to benefit investors, management, and local people living in the area where business development is to take place.

Studies have revealed that many managers lack vision, depth and training and are weak communicators locked into traditional thinking. Management is essentially about communication of meanings; this requires the ability to listen to other voices and ensure one has understood the way they perceive an issue. Listening is the starting point of all communication and problem-solving. Whilst many managers are reasonably good at technical skills, such as computing or accounting, they are weak at listening to the ideas of others and consequently their management skills suffer (Karpin, 1994, cited by Denys Delaney in written commentary on this material).

Despite the managerialist critique of top-down control systems, government and nongovernment sectors and citizens do have to make the most of environmental resources, in order not to squander them and to ensure that by saving *everyone benefits*, not just the "haves". If the basis for saving is not to profit the "haves" at the expense of the "have nots", then generic managerialist skills could be adapted whilst bearing in mind that there are no prizes for increasing the size of the budget deficit. Managerialist tools can be adapted for reflexive management, as opposed to top-down management, geared at facilitating changes to the benefit all. Participatory management styles can be enhanced by using thinking tools to ensure that all the stakeholders' perceptions are understood.

The Taylorist or scientific management approach tends to regain popularity in times of economic recession. Even if the shift away from participatory styles is not complete, hybrid forms exist with the emphasis shifting according to personalities and socio-economic factors. The economic rationalist prerogative is to maximise profits but the systemic impact on the environment and people needs to be borne in mind: "For effective risk management to take place, people, technology and business issues all need to be taken into account, and the key influence of human error must be recognised" (Wilhelmij et al. 1995:58). Further, as Beck (1992) argues, technological risks have wide-ranging social consequences but paradoxically the context for risky decision-making is the context of power imbalances. Like Foucault, Beck argues that power and knowledge are linked. Knowledge leads to risk minimisation for the rich, but he argues that if our exploitation of the environment persists, multi-nationals and corrupt governments need to realise that minimising risks is essential for the long term survival of the ecosystem. For example: Wilhelmij's, et al. (1995) project, called 'life track', is holistic and 'systems-oriented' and uses pictorial representation in flow-chart format. This is to ensure that members of work teams in high-risk petrochemical industries understand the wide-ranging ramifications of action in one part of the process. The organisation is mapped into the wider socio-environment.

Further work could be done to map the socio-anthropological aspects of the system (Wilhelmij, et al., 1996). This one project shows graphically the ecological nature of work within the environment. In industries with high risks to the environment and people, a holistic approach to analysing interactions is vital. People, the environment and economics are interlinked. But the socio-cultural and political context is often overlooked with disasterous resluts, in the bid to extract profit. Bhopal, India (Beck, 1992:44) and the environmental disasters caused by BHP in Papua New Guinea are just two examples. By tapping into the insider knowledge that workers and citizens share, both the private and public sectors could benefit. Dialogue and listening, rather than top-down approaches, can achieve success in business.

Giddens (1995) undertakes a wide-ranging critique of historical materialism. Aspects of the historical materialist analysis of the division of labour and the labour process do contribute to our understanding of the nature and origins of industrial disputes, but provide few relevant answers for today's problems. An application of paradigm dialogue could empower managers and workers alike. **EH is a tool of inquiry, understanding and action** for all global citizens who are engaged in working in all sectors of society. We need to work *with* structures not merely *within* them. EH assumes the creative potential of people and their ability to maintain or regain democratic rights. In this sense it is an optimistic approach. Despite the limitations of structure, people can and do re-create their worlds.

The theory and practice of EH are reactions to extreme forms of cultural relativity or constructivism following from postmodernist arguments that lead to a nihilistic and alienated stance about the nature of truth and social justice. It is informed by approaches that have attempted to understand the voice of the other (Fine in Denzin and Lincoln, 1994). The power imbalances of any relationship need to be addressed if 'power with' relations are to be established.

Citizens who accept an E.H. approach understand that:

(1) Social, political and economic structures shape the life chances of individuals and groups, but empowerment is rooted in the reflection of possibilities as well as action to avoid the extremes of individualism or collectivism.
(2) People have creative potential and the right to express their point of view because it would be of benefit to all. Dialogue and debate, without excessive domination of one party over the other at the organisational level and amongst stakeholders, can be extremely positive for all concerned. Interpersonal communication has the potential for creating positive alliances.

Tools for Managing Diversity Through Paradigm Dialogue

> I believe in rationality and the possibility of calling upon reason, without worshipping its goddess. . . (Castells, 1996:4)

The EH approach is optimistic about the potential of human beings to think rationally. It has not abandoned this crucial modernist or enlightenment assumption. In this sense it has drawn on the humility of postmodernism without lapsing into the cynicism of postmodern nihilism. Technology has evolved so far that human beings can create life (plant, animal and human) through genetic engineering. Human beings can create artificial worlds in closed environments that provide a potential for the colonisation of space. Would it be hubris to say that people are becoming godlike? The crisis in the world economy indicates that technocratic rationalist thinking has been inappropriate in the long term. The danger is that technological literacy and power have outstripped our theoretical literacy and ability to think systemically about the ethical implications of our socio-environmental decisions. **The potential for destruction remains, as long as we are unable to think systemically about our paradoxical *separate* rights but *shared* responsibilities.**

Caring and social justice are two sides of the same coin, namely citizenship rights, on the one hand, and citizenship responsibilities, on the other hand. These have to be balanced, in order to prevent social chaos. Thinking tools can help us avoid the binary oppositional thinking inherent in the tendency to polarise individualism and collectivism. The human condition is rooted in the paradox that we need the right to individual freedom, as much as we need the collective responsibility to societal norms that constitutes social justice. Too frequently these themes are divided. Social psychologists such as Piaget and Kohlburg (Larrabee, 1993) have argued that the contextual, relativist thinking associated with individual rights is more likely to be characteristic of women, who are carers within the private world of home and family. On the other hand, absolutist, law-based moral thinking is based on social justice concerns associated with the public, masculine sphere, which is rational as opposed to emotive in nature.

Sociologists and anthropologists have also tried to fit this oppositional grid on developed, modern and less-developed, traditional societies. The work of Carol Gilligan on moral reasoning characterised these *carers* versus *social justice* themes in terms of male and female. She has stressed in her chapter "reply to critics" (Larrabee, 1993) that she did not intend to make a causal connection between gender and type of moral reasoning, she merely wished to show that trends emerged that could be gender-linked.

The point of raising this discussion is to emphasise how much effort can be spent in debate based on binary oppositional thinking. The tendency to develop oppositional categories has plagued Western thinking. The competitive, individualist streak has been positively selected—to use Darwinian terms—in a capitalist environment. These characteristics need to be complemented with collaborative behavioural styles.

Well-known decision-making and planning tools, usually associated with top-down management styles, can be effectively adapted to suit participatory management styles if practised, for example, in focus groups and combined with listening skills. The use of the familiar "SWOT" analysis for outlining strengths, weaknesses, opportunities and threats can be worthwhile for decision-making, provided these constructs are carried out by all stakeholders and not undertaken in a top-down manner. Lewin's (1946) Force Field Analysis technique is valuable for assessing pros and cons of particular options and for ascertaining who holds these perceptions and why. The project facilitators need to understand the so-called "driving forces" and "restraining forces". It is useful to use Lewin's technique to assess who is for or against a change. Once these have been mapped out, they can be discussed using groupwork techniques. Groups with different interests may need to meet separately. Options for all the participant stakeholders could be extended through further dialogue. Understanding the conceptual maps of the stakeholders enhances the likelihood of achieving win-win solutions.

The creation of feedback loops across groups is essential for risk management. The stories and ideas of participants from different groups are recorded and shared with other groups. Their responses in the form of criticisms and agreements are noted and once again these are shared until some areas of integration emerge. This forms the basis for cooperative action. By checking out the decisions of the various groups and by comparing them with one another, the facilitator could find that one group tries to dominate the decisions of other interest groups! Once the facilitator has information from all the groups, it is possible to elect representatives from each to work for a viable win-win solution for all. Mary Parker Follett used this concept in the 1920s and it was used in 1991 by Fisher and Ury. Dana (1990) also explored the process of both-win negotiation and has pointed out that the initiative will not always succeed if power differences are too great and parties involved in negotiation are irrational, in so far as they can see only one viewpoint for whatever reason. A decision is only effective if it represents the wishes of all the participants.

Dialogue to create common denominators across interest groups is part of the challenge. It is by means of exploring options and reflecting on the consequences that problems can be addressed constructively. Hersey and Blanchard (1988) relate decision-making to different styles of management that are in turn linked with the four "readiness levels of the followers", namely: "directing, persuading, participating and delegating". It is necessary for managers to facilitate the participation of the followers and they should strive for their inclusion in decision-making through involvement. People skills are based on listening to the other's construct of a situation. This approach has great relevance to the way we do research and to diversity management. Focus-group discussions can be used for research to find out the needs of all participants and evaluate information to solve problems in project management, for example, or help groups make decisions.

According to Hettne (1995:77) qualitative research such as ethnography and participatory action research requires listening to the way informants' frame or construct their world. Ethnographers, ideally, try to represent the view of informants without imposing the researcher's frame of reference, but in fact, many early ethnographers did impose their biases. Today qualitative research strives to avoid the 'colonial top down approach' and managers would do well to avoid these mistakes. Participatory Action Research methods or 'learning whilst doing' provide an alternative way to obtain information. Trying out solutions with people who actively help frame the questions, provides a different way of seeing, understanding and solving problems.

The qualitative research process is not necessarily without pitfalls. For instance, the meanings of informants contribute to shaping research data and the researcher's presence causes reactivity, even if this is reduced over time as trust builds. But as trust builds, the emotional content of the relationship can also increase. Qualitative research draws on and is informed by feminist research (Patricia Hill Collins 1989 in Fonow and Cook 1991) because understanding meaning is central to qualitative research and does not ignore emotional aspects. The focus group discussion can be used as a decision-making process that strives to feed back information across groups or individuals. Once ideas are generated they are shared with the next individual or group; they are considered and suggestions are added. This is an iterative, sharing process that can lead to the generation of common denominators.

The Nominal Group technique (Baron 1986:411) is used for problem-solving in a way not too dissimilar from brainstorming. Unlike brainstorming, ideas are generated anonymously reducing potential for conflict within the group (Tyson, 1989). Conducting focus group discussions, as a successful means of generating creative solutions to problems, requires basic skills in group dynamics.

Bureaucracies Have Been the Organisational Forms Used to Address All Aspects of Life: Work, Education, Health, Welfare and Government

If we spend a day at the coalface of human-service delivery and throw up our hands in despair, arguing it is impossible to deal with the ripple effects of change—starting with global markets and working inward to national and then local interests—we will achieve little. It is essential to think in terms of the *interconnectedness* of social problems and achieve the intellectual dexterity to see the connections and avoid thinking in terms of categories or boxes. At least this will enable us to see what we can do to address the bigger picture.

For example, the public-housing sector is impacted by management and labour-force decisions, which are in turn shaped by economists and governments. To achieve common goals, the only way to deal with the big picture is tracing the links and working out how best to impact policies through collaboration across sectors and through wide-ranging social movements that span the apparent differences in interest groups. In this context problem solving at all times needs to avoid pinning down, limiting, categorising and refining down. Fuzziness is unavoidable.

Problem-solving using a narrow focus is inappropriate in today's globalizing economy and society. No matter whether we are social analysts or citizens attempting to make sense of the world, we cannot operate merely at the micro level. For example, if our concern is cutbacks in the public-housing stock for the most needy, as governments move from universal to residual welfare, we must understand how shifts in wider markets impact on local economies. For instance, we have: 1) the need for a mobile workforcep; 2) a flexible contracted workforce with little long-term job security and a sense of being too intimidated to complain about their work conditions; and 3) fluctuations in interest rates that could curtail the confidence of the low-income would-be homeowner. All these considerations—pertaining to the links between personal life chances and political realities—shape life-styles, development opportunities and welfare considerations. Most importantly, these concerns are not narrow or disparate; they are interlinked and require practical intervention at a number of levels and sectors.

The consequences of fragmentation for development and democracy will be explored by drawing on the principles of the WHO Ottawa Health Charter, which emphasise the need for systemic thinking for problem-solving in the linked domains of health and development in order to achieve sustainable life-styles.

Social justice in the public sphere and care in the private sphere (Gilligan, 982 and Larrabee, 1993) can be better served by connectedness and lateral thinking rather than "either or thinking". Paradigm dialogue can be used to explore boundaries and overlaps amongst people who have different life chances.

Education, Research and Knowledge Creation

Let's consider knowledge creation in the "halls of academe". "Publish or perish" is the well-worn phrase with dire implications for academics who spend hours doing worthwhile creative work and have a low output in quantitative terms, as well as for those who achieve no output at all! The global context cannot be ignored because it shapes most aspects of university life and has an impact on knowledge creation and dissemination. Economic rationalism has become institutionalised in university policy and practice. Meeting the needs of industry and establishing links with industry lend further weight to the so-called 'competency approach' to teaching and learning. 'Quality teaching' in this context is translated into meeting the needs of industry and ensuring that students obtain work at the end of their increasingly expensive courses.

Both the latter goals of meeting industry needs and extending boundaries of knowledge are reasonable, provided the university encourages creative, 'liberative' thinking rather than pragmatic, technocratic thinking that meets the ends of industry alone. The university system in the developed Western world has not had a track record of ensuring that the latter goal—liberative thinking—has been achieved in the past. The old notion of academics being "objective" because they are part of a university system and not the private sector is becoming increasingly blurred. Whether or not academics were ever objective is debatable. The dominant discourse was always the one most functional to the ruling elites rather than 'the other', who differed in class, cultural, racial, political, gender or health terms. Categorical thinking is useful for conservative politics because it has "a go no further effect" (Zola, 1975). In medicine, for example, the notion of concentrating on clinical conditions of a disease and focusing on the individual rather than the social context is also a political model; it can be used to shift blame away from the public to the private context and can lead to victim blaming.

The Context of Teaching, Learning and Working

Let's consider the context of teaching and learning. Making the education system, and the university system in particular, accountable to the employment needs of students and industry is not necessarily a bad thing—if the needs of these stakeholders are not out of kilter with other stakeholders and the environment. What does this mean for ethical practice? Who is the "master we should serve"? Are we to become "handmaidens" of industry and, at the same time, develop lifelong learning skills amongst our students whilst doing meaningful work and publishing? This is the challenge. "Both and thinking" not "either or thinking" is essential, but the question is: in whose interests? Serving industry is of little value if the interests of all citizens and the environment are not placed first.

The competency approach must be understood in the context of cutbacks. Lists of competencies pertaining to industry sectors have considerable appeal, in so far as they provide guidelines for best practice, but not unless they are counterbalanced with a revival of critical and creative thinking skills (McIntyre, 1995; 1996). The purpose of this discussion is to reflect on the implications of the teaching and learning environment on the way we think and do research. The following quotation concerning social work in Australia has wider relevance for knowledge creation and practice: "Current pressures from the social work profession and employers to increase the emphasis on 'hard' skills at the expense of developing the student's capacity to challenge existing orthodoxies need to be resisted" (Meekosha and Mowbray, 1990:343). They argue that a technical bag of tricks cannot replace an ability to think analytically, critically and reflexively. A more recent quotation draws a direct link among competency, effectiveness and efficiency, i.e., productivity in economic rationalist terms. "Competency", to paraphrase Kalantzis (1992:5) is a measurement of what people can do rather than what they know. Further: "As the great engine of economic rationalism churns on, it is little wonder that innovation in post-compulsory education should be almost exclusively about work skills. Education at this level it seems, is really only of interest insofar as it prepares students to be productive workers. Reading both the Finn and Mayer reports, and the Carmichael Report. . . it is hard not to get this impression".

The purpose of this section is, **firstly,** to argue that styles of learning need to be changed if we are to achieve a sense of global citizenship rights and responsibilities. **Secondly**, I argue that the process for teaching deep, as opposed to superficial, learning skills is the basis of learning how to become a global citizen.

Bateson (1972) identified learning at three levels. There is a progression from Level 1, a type of rote learning, to Level 2, at which people are able to apply frameworks to different contexts, to Level 3, at which people are able to compare and contrast different frameworks. For instance, a schoolchild may be taught about citizenship rights and responsibilities in Australia in the following ways:

The teacher hands out a list of civic rights and responsibilities and the children are asked to learn the list for a test at the end of the week. No discussion of the "fact sheet" is invited. This is learning at the lowest level (Level 1). Alternatively the same set of children may be asked to consider the list of civic rights and responsibilities and ask their parents and grandparents how this list has changed during their lifetime because of the changing social, political and economic context. The children are asked to record what is said about the list, report to the class, and then write an essay once they have heard responses from all their classmates. This is learning at Level 2, because the framework of current citizenship rights and responsibilities is compared across time within one context.

Another way of learning would be to ask the children what it means to be a citizen and what they consider to be social rights and responsibilities as, for example young Australians who are not as yet eligible to vote. The class could be asked to consider their expectations of social justice in Australia in comparison with other places in the world. The class could then be asked to compare and contrast the frameworks of citizenship. This is Level 3 learning.

The global environment and her people are at risk because although we are technically literate, we continue to be theoretically illiterate. Consequently, technology is not used to liberate human beings but to oppress some in the interest of others. This is the product of a world in which modes of production have shaped particular styles of ontology and epistemology.

By choosing to think that explanation is only possible on the basis of positivist laws of cause and effect established on the basis of experimental designs, we limit our ability to find complex solutions to social and environmental problems. These require lateral thinking, not narrow types of deduction and induction. It cannot be denied that a place exists for this sort of thinking, just that we need to do other types of thinking too, namely holistic or 'systemic thinking'. As global citizens, we have a right and responsibility to find ways to create common denominators, not barriers. Citizenship needs to be understood in terms of private and public rights and responsibilities of thinking, feeling human beings who by virtue of their humanity (mind and body), have much in common but by virtue of their specific life experiences, have individual needs and potential.

For too long, academia has worked according to an adversarial system in which proving our favoured theory right was often based on proving others wrong. This was done rather than emphasising the ways in which other theories stimulated new thought. As Gouldner (1971) suggested, we need to find the liberative potential in theories and 'interpolate across paradigms to find common areas' (Flood and Romm, 1996). The adversarial system of thinking permeates all our institutions: education, religion, political policy, law and the industrial sector.

The arena for citizens who wish to maintain hard-won citizenship rights is not merely the voting booth. As we have seen in many democracies, the party political system represents similar versions of New Right thinking. In order to create wider options, we need to find and create new social movement arenas through which to bring about wide-ranging cultural changes. A vital arena for change is "the self", changing the way in which we think through learning openness to other ways of framing reality and listening skills. It certainly may not be our fault that we are, at best, technically literate and, generally speaking, theoretically illiterate. After we have blamed our rigid, simplistic thinking on the schools and what pass for universities and places of technical learning—shaped by politicians and economists—we still have to rely on our human creativity to solve problems in our immediate lives.

Old-fashioned notions of citizenship associated with bounded sets of rights and responsibilities are no longer as applicable as they were before. The arenas for practising citizenship—lobbying and social action have changed. The old arenas—groups, organisations, parties and bureaucracies—on the whole focused on single issues. The new arenas have a multiple focus. They include all the above arenas and attempt to:

- change the way we model the definition of problems, using thinking tools for creative approaches to find the liberative potential in many models;
- use technology for regular, fast response to identified problems, not merely voting;
- network to create corporate solutions by forging links across government, nongovernment, business and labour sectors through finding common denominators;
- create matrices for working on common goals;
- create social movements at local (regional), national and international levels.

Knowledge and power have long been seamlessly connected; the dominant culture determines what constitutes appropriate communication in terms of language, accent, vocabulary and social manners. *The content of knowledge has reflected the social, political and economic needs and values of the dominant sectors of society within the nation state.* Similarly, powerful interest groups within nation states have determined the value of Indigenous knowledge as lesser and subject to modification (read improvement) by the powerful. The shift in thinking in some academic sectors to respect the personal knowledge of the less powerful has come about as a result of postmodern thinking, which emphasises that modern, enlightenment thinking has not come up with all the answers and that, in fact, it has produced many problems. Pollution and over-exploitation of the world's resources are just two of the most obvious examples; the third is hubris, an overweening pride in the technological prowess of the West. A realisation that perhaps there is more than one way of seeing, leads to a realisation that when doing problem-solving there may be more than one answer. The privileging of more than one voice is only possible when dialogue is maintained. The assumption that truth is dialogue leads to a realisation that if global knowledge is to be a goal of research and problem-solving, then the tension between local diversity and common denominators is our goal.

For instance, **modernist** solutions were based on a particular understanding of the nature of the problem, the nature of science, and the role of citizens. In **postmodern, postindustrial society,** we are faced with social and environmental risks that can only be addressed through problem-solving approaches that address multiple variables. The nature of a problem can only be understood by exploring it through the eyes of those who are experiencing, discussing and defining it. Problem-solving can only begin when the nature of the problem has been read and interpreted by all stakeholders who voice their contextual understanding of issues embedded in their lived experiences. Consequently, when we are thinking about methods for solving problems, we need to ensure that they are participatory and not 'top down'. The way we understand the nature of a problem will shape the way in which we go about trying to solve the problem. The first step in solving problems is understanding the way in which different groups define the problem. The next step is to help all stakeholders understand how 'the other' defines the problem. The third step is to realise that all paradigms could teach us something, and all paradigms have potential strengths and weaknesses. This humility is the starting point for creating new knowledges that are both *global* and *local* in content. This interpretation of postmodernism embraces and respects diversity through being open to many voices. It does not lapse into cynical nihilism.

Meta-theories are not the best solution; instead, developing an understanding of diversity, without blueprinting a single solution, is considered preferable. In this respect the argument differs from Bateson's (1972) work, *Steps to an Ecology of Mind,* that identifies thinking meta-theoretically as the highest order of knowledge. We require intellectual dexterity rooted in respect for the contextual, creative potential of human beings.

To sum up, by choosing to think that explanation is only possible on the basis of positivist laws of cause and effect established on the basis of experimental designs, we limit our ability to find complex solutions to social problems. Multi-semic thinking, tracing systems that bind all human beings to survival in a common global environment, releases human beings from simplistic, hemmed-in solutions to problems.

Multidisciplinary and Intersectoral Approach to Health Promotion

In a preface to *Autopoiesis: The Organisation of the Living* by Maturana and Varela (1973), Stafford Beer summarises the meaning of autopoiesis:

> Science is ordered knowledge. It began with classification. . . . It is a worldview in which real systems are annihilated in trying to understand them, in which relations are lost, because they are not categorised, in which synthesis is relegated to poetry and mysticism, in which identity is a political inference. We may inspect the result of the structure and organisation of the contemporary university. . .It is an iron maiden, in whose secure embrace scholarship is trapped. For many, this is an entirely satisfactory situation, just because the embrace is secure. A man (sic) can lay claim to knowledge about some categorised bit of the world, however tiny, which is greater than anyone else's knowledge of that bit, is safe for life: reputation grows, paranoia deepens. The number of papers increases exponentially, knowledge grows by infinitesimals, but understanding of the world actually recedes, because the world really is an interacting system. And since the world, in many of its aspects, is changing at an exponential rate, this kind of scholarship, rooted in the historical search of its own sanctified categories, is in large part unavailing to the needs of mankind. . .

Systemic thinking would help to promote better health but thinking is bound to disciplinary bases and these bases are used for defining competencies for practice. The end result is that development work is segmented, and hence the exhortation made by the Ottawa Health Charter of 1986 to see the links between health and development and to work in a multi-disciplinary and intersectoral manner. The problem is that this approach merely responds to the effects of dividing knowledge into compartments, rather than seeing the interconnections from the outset. The problem-solving potential of a discipline-based approach is limited because of competition amongst disciplines rather than cooperation and collaboration. This competitive sectarianism in thinking reflects the economic rationalist environment in which we operate.

An integrated approach to understanding the world could lead to improved social measures to promote social heath and prevent problems from occurring. Physical, mental and spiritual well-being can only occur when people live in harmony with themselves, others and their environment. When this does not occur, crime, mental disorders, pollution, wars, industrial disasters, and exploitative economic systems come into being.

Of course there is a need to focus or specialise but not in the way in which it currently occurs. We need to teach people to interpolate across disciplines, not think in terms of separate territories. To help solve complex problems together, whether she or he differs in terms of culture or profession, we need to realise that definitions of problems and solutions are based on deeply held assumptions about the world (Geddes in Geddes, Hughes and Remenyi, 1994).

When assumptions are out of alignment, paradigm dialogue can help participants understand the implications of these assumptions for people and their environment. Within cultures, gender, age, personal and material resources can be ascribed very different meanings. The challenge for a global citizen is, on the one hand, to develop or retain right-hemisphere lateral and holistic thinking without resorting to postmodern doubt. On the other hand, it is to realise that the social world is more complex than was previously represented in neat, structural models that characterise left-hemisphere modern thinking. If we can understand that the closest we can ever get to a shared sense of 'truth' is through listening to and learning the frame of reference of the other, then the first step will be taken.

The Ottawa Health Charter of 1986 **responded to the fragmented view of the world**. The links between health and development in terms of physical, mental and spiritual well-being have received increased recognition in recent years as a result of the official ratification of the World Health Organisation. An approach that reflects on the implications of the various sets of assumptions avoids the extremes of individualism and collectivism. The self-reflexive nature of human beings is central to their humanity, and the lack of self-reflexiveness in thought and action leads to inner or interpersonal conflict. Human beings have a right and responsibility to be involved in creating and understanding their world. If we could avoid breaking down knowledge into rigid categories, then we would not need to find ways to put them together again and we would not have this ontological and epistemological debate amongst practitioners who are working in multi-disciplinary teams (Reason, 1991).

The idea that categories of specialisation can lead to more expertise in solving problems has passed. For example, an EH systemic approach to mental health promotion could be an improvement on the current approach, which is interdisciplinary rather than transdisciplinary. According to Cooper in the introduction to Foucault's *Madness and Civilization* (1967:viii–ix), the way individuals and groups respond to social problems tells one much about the nature of society.

Compartmentalisation and isolation of social problems that lead to technocratic problem-solving and control of 'the other' need to be avoided. Health promotion in terms of a systems approach would transcend categorisation. Networking and paradigm dialogue are the most vital processes for achieving a transcendence in health-care promotion and service delivery.

To use an example: If a doctor, community nurse, social worker, community youth worker, school teacher, psychologist, sociologist and biologist sat together to discuss a young person 'at risk', to use the current label, the frames of reference of the participants could be very different. The GP and biologist could be concerned about the impact of binge drinking on the young person's liver and nervous system; the psychologist could be concerned about the young person's inability to think in terms of consequences of his actions. The community nurse and social worker could be concerned about the young person's vulnerability and social isolation and the school teacher might view the young person as a liability to the class she teaches because of the disruptive role model he might set for other students. The sociologist could be concerned that this young immigrant has values that set him apart from his family and, in a bid to be part of an Australian peer group, he conforms too much to youth counter culture.

Young people who must negotiate more than one culture and cope with adolescence have particular challenges. A broader socio-cultural intervention than merely casework and counselling is required. Each of the participants sees a slice of the situation, but unfortunately not the whole. Added to this, the status differentials amongst the professional participants also shape the direction of decision-making, as do the personalities of the various participants. Assumptions and values shape the way in which we see the world and the way in which we go about researching it.

A public-health approach would need to take a preventative stance to youth alienation by working across a number of sectors and disciplines. Public-health approaches, unlike modernist approaches, do not try to isolate a single cause. Instead, an attempt is made to discover weblike causation or even simple feedback systems amongst variables.

We need thinking tools to facilitate better planning with all the stakeholders, to address the barriers between insider and outsider perceptions of what constitutes democratic problem-solving. These tools will help to identify conceptual boundaries and overlaps amongst people so as to improve project planning. These tools—when used in a focus group discussion with stakeholders from a range of disciplines—could benefit investors, managers, and local people living in the area where development is to take place.

When the mental map of one person is out of alignment with society, he is considered mad, ill, a genius, merely an eccentric, or a criminal—depending on the context. Breaking the rule is usually high-risk behaviour that can lead to negative sanctions or, less often, positive sanctions—if the gamble is successful. Negative sanctions are tied to specific contexts and are clear-cut responses to socially defined laws. The decision as to whether illegal drug users should be subjected to capital punishment, incarcerated, or treated as health victims varies greatly from one geographical and temporal context to another. Further, categories of class, race and gender come into play.

Under mandatory sentencing laws effective in 1997, a young person who steals a can of beer can be jailed, if this is a second property offence in the Northern Territory of Australia. A high-profile society woman in New South Wales can be released from a drunk-driving charge, whilst a low-status illegal drug user can simply be jailed for possession. Paradoxically, some illegal drugs are deemed very useful for palliative care; legal recreational drugs cause as much death through violence, road death and cancer as illegal drugs. The boundaries between acceptable/unacceptable, legal/illegal are indeed arbitrary, but specific sanctions in certain geographical contexts are not. A correctional services officer who accompanied me during visits at a female prison was asked the question: Are these women drug addicts in need of medical and social care, or are they criminals in need of incarceration? The answer was "both". Increased information flows will eventually make it necessary to confront paradoxes that collide with neat categories.

Shifting Communication Away From Top Down, One to One Approaches to Dialogue and Networking

One of the dangerous responses of people who feel free of previous structures of patriarchy—expressed through the institutions of the extended family and formal religions—is a sense of being lost (*The Homeless Mind,* Peter Berger et al., 1974). The sense of powerlessness has been addressed in postmodern society by shunning the global and national context and compensating for the breakdown in communities and traditional extended families by ritualising a sense of control and focusing inward. At the physical level, the body has been celebrated; individual expression in fashion and individual journeys of sexual discovery are reactions. Another reaction is the revival of self-focused spiritualism. The individual right to physical and spiritual fulfillment is served best through avoiding fundamentalist versions of religion and embracing the liberative potential of belief systems that acknowledge the value not only of "the self ", but "the other".

By shifting communication away from top-down approaches to one of dialogue and networking around multiple nodes of support, much can be done to address the "homeless mind". Amongst the most challenged carers are those providing palliative care to the dying and to those suffering mental pain and delusions. Dying and losing touch with socially defined reality are the final taboos for modern society; they present a sense of the finality of binary oppositions. Postmodern society stands in awe of these boundaries, others are considered to be permeable because postmodern society, in many cases, has destroyed the belief systems that render or translate the meaning*less*ness of life's inevitable tragedies into a meaning*ful* journey. Thus, religion can make the unbearable bearable, without merely being "an opiate of the people", as Marx argued.

The liberative potential in traditional religions is a celebration of the continuity of nature through cycles of creation, death and re-birth, which provides healing and a sense of completeness, wholeness or holiness. Systemic cyclical thinking underpins most religions in which the seasons of life, death, birth and renewal are ritually celebrated. These need to be understood rather than dismissed as recreational in a postmodern world because they are re-creational. The associated participatory rituals delimit a sense of chaos when one thinks only in terms of human time, rather than the landscape of seasons or the long time spans in the creation of earth. Religious symbols that link the human and natural world help people accept the uncontrollable as part of the cycles of nature and have played an important role in most cultures. Ritual draws together support networks within the community to express pain and hope in acts of communion. Communion through participatory dialogue and networking can promote a better quality of life and death. It provides an antidote to individualism and the location of pain within the individual by minimising it through sharing.

From indigenous healer networks in Cape Town, South Africa to palliative care-supporter networks in the Barrosa, South Australia the role of the network provides support to more marginalised, by pooling and sharing resources and giving emotional support in a respectful rather than top-down manner. The way in which communication occurs can either ameliorate or exacerbate physical and mental conditions. It would be naive at this point not to acknowledge the socio-economic context in which indigenous healers are consulted. Poverty and lack of access to medical services plus vulnerability to charlatans, who in many cases, exploit patients' trust in traditional wisdom—without a critical awareness rooted in a familiarity with scientific models—are factors that cannot be brushed aside. Nevertheless, in acknowledging the downside of indigenous healing, contributions made by sincere holistic healers, who work with bio-medical systems, should not be dismissed.

The indigenous healer network uses an autopoietic approach to healing in so far as a host of interlinked treatment approaches are adopted. Sharing food, emotional chanting and nurturing baptisms are as important as listening to their hopes and fears during dance seances, where dream symbolism is interpreted in the presence of relevant family members and close friends. They not only listen to the voices of those who are troubled, but provide a polyrhythmic musical accompaniment by clapping to the drums. The initiates, led by the diviner mother, form an inner dancing circle; family and friends sit around the outer circumference of a circle. Drumming, clapping and chanting induce an altered state of consciousness.

When initiate are ready to share their dreams, the diviner mother raises the dancing stick and the silence is filled with their words, "The ancestors say. . . ." In this way their words have authority; the ancestors are more senior in the lineage than any living kin but they remain linked with them and intimately involved in their daily lives. The continuity between life and death is emphasised in African cosmology. Their words are acknowledged by the mantra "Camagu. . ." meaning, in this context, "Amen" or "thanks be in the name of the ancestors". The affirmation of the continuity of the life cycle is thus absolute.

The power of the diviner network is that membership through sickness opens up access to people who are on the same journey. Group work, dream analysis, and listening to the point of view of the sufferer in an accepting and nonjudgmental manner are the healing methods used to apply to all the senses: hearing, sight, taste, touch. Time is given to the sufferer not only within the ritual context but also on an ongoing day-to-day basis, where nurturing includes both counselling and laughter. The richness of the experience cannot be portrayed in this brief summary of some of the elements of healing: listening to the words of the initiates; symbols to mark each stage of healing; herbal washes and medicines; healing tools such as the dancing stick; a tail of a cow, which symbolises potency, wealth and status; and the sacrifice of an animal to commune with ancestors—symbolising the paradox of life, that in death there is life. There is also the presence of family and friends; sharing of meat (valuable protein); sustained emotional support; release of tension through dance, chanting and smoking a hallucinogenic plant; laughter; and drinking a quantity of maize beer, which is both intoxicating and rich in vitamins. The symbols emphasise harmony with one's fellow human beings and nature. Berger (1997) argues that laughter is spiritual and cathartic, because humour explores the paradoxes of life ironically and thus removes the sting.

The sharing that occurs during the ritual is not only with the diviner mother but also with fellow initiates who are also facing a personal crisis and relevant family or friends who have an interest in their well-being. If the initiate is isolated then they rely on the network of members in the diviner network. Ideally the diviner has qualified to be a healer of others because he or she has also been through the process of sickness and healing. There is a sense of empathy as a result of personal experience, this is illustrated by the response made by diviners who say in response to their initiates' stories: "I feel your pain".

Some indigenous healers are more sincere than others and some are charlatans, in so far as they are motivated only by profit and have a linked knowledge of Indigenous healing practices; nevertheless, the ideal healer can teach many lessons. There is a sense of optimism that the sickness is a journey that marks the beginning of a calling sent by ancestors who, beyond the barrier of death, continue to have a particular interest in their living kin. The symptoms of illness are regarded as a message from ancestors, who send the sickness as a sign initiates need to apprentice themselves to a diviner to learn to heal themselves and then others. As such, the process is empowering and initiates at the onset of their symptoms, are paradoxically regarded as vulnerable but also potentially powerful. They symbolise their mental and physical vulnerability by wearing white.

Anyone who understands African cosmology understands the symbolism of being an 'umkwetha' or initiate. Wearing white symbolises the status of the wearer as being liminal or in transition and undergoing a rite of passage (Van Gennep, 1960). Liminality is seen as powerful and is not stigmatised as mental disorders continue to be by Western psychology and psychiatry. The interpretation of dreams by the igqira is not undertaken in order to diagnose and control, but to make sense of pain and to enable the initiate to move to the next spiritual level. There is no split between the patient and the doctor. It is accepted that the sick will become healers of others and the sickness is a journey of empowerment to understanding the pain of others.

The sickness is both the message and the route to becoming a carer of others. As a result of having suffered, the carer understands the pain of others. Thus compassion stems from the experience of pain and the optimism gained from having moved through pain to a state of grace in harmony with one's environment, self, ancestral shades, and living kin. The stages of healing are marked by ritual and supported by fellow initiates;

such group therapy, rich in symbolism, continues to be a meaningful option in modern society.

Let us compare this indigenous healing model with the Western biomedical paradigm. Intwaso, or "the possession state" or "calling" provides a cultural idiom more positive than the Western notion of a "mental breakdown", a label that holds stigma rather than potency!

In Western society the mad are controlled by drugs and/or physical separation and stigmatised for their lack of rationality. Definitions of madness and badness reflect the sociocultural, political and economic context in which powerful professionals and doctors make their diagnoses. Few Western thinkers accept that madness can, in many instances, be "a sane response to an insane world" (Laing, 1960; Boyers and Orril, 1972). The lack of respect for the dignity of 'the other' is partly because of the need to think in terms of categories of right and wrong, with little respect for diversity from the socially accepted norm. The relevance of other variables such as biochemistry and genetics besides the social, is not denied, nor is the place of clinical treatment in some contexts.

Carers schooled in Western positivism, through the years, have worked in the top-down manner of "the expert who knows best". As years have past, the modernisation/top-down approaches in human-service and welfare work have been augmented by approaches stressing the point of view of those who are "at the mercy or behest of state welfare or international development transfers"—which may or may not be paving the way for multi-nationals or other powerful interest groups. Not surprisingly the language of "care and understanding" has been added sincerely and less sincerely at the dictates of policy and personality. Cynicism in the field of health, welfare and development seems forgivable given its track record.

A palliative carers' support network (Elsey and McIntyre, 1996) in a nonmetropolitan area of South Australia provides a

model of a development initiative built up around mentors who provide information and ongoing support to the dying and those caring for the dying. Carers dealing with the silenced areas of death, dying and mental health need the opportunity to share their burden and compare stories, so as to heal themselves and learn how to help 'the other'. Carers who have not suffered any personal trauma may not be able to understand the world view of 'the other'. Respecting their assumptions about the nature of reality is the starting point for all healing.

Practical information on pain management for carers, through using a host of clinical and socio-emotive means, was discussed regularly by means of a video and phone linkup. The project embraced the liberative potential of information technology for communicating and healing, whilst bearing in mind that it is no replacement for face-to-face communion. The technology augmented and empowered those who worked in geographical space.

The network tried out a simple conversational model to address the specific needs of palliative carers, but it could serve equally well to assist members of the community in need of a range of support services. Information was not shared in a top-down way; instead, the small things that carers did were affirmed—from placing flowers on the tray of a dying person, to the value of friendship, music and animals. It was acknowledged that pain, both physical and mental, could be given different meanings depending on the context of the suffering. This, it was agreed, could be substantially eliminated through combining drug therapy with a range of alternative healing options. Experts from the Flinders Pain Management Clinic endorsed the wisdom of ordinary people and gave details on how to work with clinical nurses to manage drug therapy.

Rapport created through video conferencing and phone support cannot replace face-to-face caring and nurturing. How-

ever, it can help create communities of shared concern to augment limited support available in geographical communities affected by costcutting and lack of services.

Tools to aid negotiated discourses between 'the researcher'/ carer/development facilitator and 'the other' are urgently required. Greene in Denzin and Lincoln (1994:541) discusses the need 'to privilege', rather than subordinate, the other when undertaking communication geared to researching needs and developing policy

It is clear that authorities are usually interested at the point of the cycle at which a set of behaviours can be called 'a social problem'. Much attention in Alice Springs has been focused on the results of marginalisation—high rates of alcohol use and public drinking—rather than the causes, namely a sense of being treated as second-class citizens.[6]

Some of the key issues facing Aboriginal people in Central Australia are: high rates of unemployment and mandatory sentencing rules— leading to the highest incarceration rates and suicide rates nationally.[7] Coping with grief and sadness is a central concern for a community that is worse off in terms of the social indicators—incarceration, suicide, poor school retention rates, unemployment, morbidity and mortality rates.

Bowden (1994) emphasises the way Aboriginal youth culture is used by young people for resistance against both their parents and wider society. This is a source of great difficulty for young people and the social outcomes indicate. High-risk behaviour is the way in which young people cope with a sense of being powerless. Providing a voice for marginalised young people through creativity and community development projects enables young people to demonstrate what citizenship rights and responsibility really mean. These are important ways to bring about social healing, because these methods help to raise self-esteem and sense of being in control of life. Active commu-

nity approaches which address social causes across sectors and disciplines need to augment passive one-to-one counselling and measures which address the effects not the causes of social problems.

6

Class, Culture and Sustainable Global Democracy

Power, politics and life chances

> Complexity thinking should be considered as a method for understanding diversity, rather than a unified meta-theory. Its epistemological value could come from acknowledging the serendipitous nature of Nature and of society. Not that there are no rules, but that rules are created, and changed, in a relentless process of deliberate actions and unique interactions. The information technology paradigm does not evolve towards its closure as a system, but its openness as a multi-edged network. . . . (Castells, 1996:65).

Space and time have been altered by culture, but the ecological imperatives remain. Bureaucracies are shifting towards matrices and fluid structures in response to the fluid fast-changing economy, where borders no longer provide buffers so reactions have to be fast. As Toffler (1990) outlined in *Power Shift*, the change from cubbyhole thinking to systems thinking or network thinking will require changes in the way societies are organised. Space is no longer merely local and neighbourhood-based; communication through interactive technology has created close links with the national and international domains. Cyberspace has effectively impacted on local space, but people cannot dictate the imperatives of the environment unless they wish to experience pollution, erosion and climatic disasters.

Castells (1997) argues that it is through the flows of information in cyberspace that the real power lies, because it is more powerful than that wielded by state bureaucracies. This is partially true, but the power of cyberspace needs to be harnessed to benefit local groups in geographical human space.

Changes in organisational structures have positive and negative outcomes. For ordinary people the shift from working in highly supervised and closely managed bureaucracies to working in flatter, leaner organisations, that strive to be flexible in response to changing markets, is often disorientation or, worse, a shift from full-time employment to contract work and the loss of the right to plan financially. Down-sizing and the increased use of technology result in higher ratios of unemployment and under-employment at a time when the welfare states in the West are cutting back. The likelihood is that standards of living will be threatened by the need to compete in a global economy in which long-term "protectionism" continues to be frowned upon, despite the collapse of economies in Asia in 1998.

Racist responses to immigrants and refugees are indicative of the usual socio-political response to economic threats. This impacts on the notion of democracy and work. The ordinary working and middle class have demonstrated their fears through New Right and nationalistic movements in parts of the world where welfare states are under threat. For instance, in the late 1990s there was a ground swell of racism in Australia against First Australians and Asian immigrants. New Right groups forged a conservative social movement to support the political party "One Nation" led by Pauline Hanson. Scapegoating particular groups provides a simplistic response to complex issues, namely: 'blame the other'.

The liberative potential of flexible organisations needs to be preserved without the downside of dismantling the achievements of workers' rights. Only lobbying through social move-of being able to afford education and later command the salaries of professionals.

Even though crude access to capital is not the only way to succeed in the fast-changing, information-led economy, it is certainly one of the keys to success. A capitalist who is out of touch with information systems will lose market share, as will a capitalist who has a rigid organisational philosophy that does not respond quickly to shifting markets.

A shift from crude analysis of class being "access to the means of production"—when modified in the Weberian sense to include status components—remains relevant; this is particularly true if status is considered in cultural terms. Bourdieu's work argues that class is the basis for cultural differences (Crook, Pakulski, et al., 1993) for instance, in art, music, attitudes towards education and social interaction. He calls this 'cultural capital' and he does not dislocate it from class. It can be argued, however, that if one accepts that each so-called class/cultural position has a contribution to make, then the value of found objects—wire turned by children into art works, indigenous songs, chants, and music in regional dialects—would be valued for the cultural diversity they can bring to the so-called mainstream of art and culture.

In this sense, Bourdieu also differs a little from Waters (1995), who argues that it is at the level of **consumption** that classes differ: ". . .in a culturalized global economy, world class is displaced by a world status system based on consumption, lifestyle and value commitment" (p. 95). "This is not to suggest, however, that economic stratification has disappeared from the face of the earth. Rather that the stratification pattern is now focussed on possibilities for consumption rather than production relations. The emerging pattern is indeed an international one, in which members of rich societies, even if they are unemployed, tend to enjoy significantly better consumption possibilities than employees in developing societies. . . . ."(pp. 92-93).

Instead of the crude notion of bourgeoisie and petit bourgeoisie capitalists versus the proletariat and lumpenproletariat in Marx's analysis, we need to think in terms of complex stratification based on a fluid set of indices that reflect the socio, political and economic environment of the ascribers and the ascribed. The implications of being at the top or bottom of the stratification heap in developed and developing countries are important in so far as the standard of living of the *unemployed, who have access to universal benefits provided by a welfare state,* would be better off than the *unemployed,* who have access only to *residual benefits in a contracting welfare state,* and the *unemployed who have no access to benefits because state welfare in a so-called third world or less-developed country is unavailable,* would have the lowest life chances.

The problem is that in a changing world where state responsibility for citizens is contracting, the likelihood is that the unemployed could become increasingly marginalised in both developed and less-developed regions, unless citizens strive to maintain and regain democratic gains in multiple arenas. It is no coincidence that the pockets of poverty found in so-called developed countries mirror the same social and demographic characteristics as those found in undeveloped countries. The infant mortality rates in the slums of Boston and New York are not dissimilar to those in rural South Africa or, for that matter rural Aboriginal Australia.

According to Chomsky (1993), the "Third World" and "First World"are not as separate as we are led to think. The dynamic of exploitation of the have nots by haves should not be clouded by postmodernist relativism of what constitutes 'truth', because class is alive and well and mutating to suit the new environment! Postmodernism can serve capitalism well if it leads to the sort of extreme relativism that undermines the identification of rights and responsibilities! Human rights are a global concern. A key stumbling block that needs to be borne in mind is that as practitioners working in the global economy shaped by economic rationalism, we do not forget the importance of understanding the links amongst power, culture and knowledge. We need to become global citizens as opposed to citizens inspired by national interests, in order to maintain or regain democratic rights embedded in social justice principles. Social justice concerns are global not local. Succumbing to bourgeoisie self-interest in this new era of economic rationalism has far-reaching implications for people and the environment.

> Extreme and public violations of human rights often meet with widespread global condemnation and frequently with multinational political action. Among the more notable examples we can mention the patchy though effective economic, sporting and cultural sanctions against the white racist regimes of Rhodesia (Zimbabwe) and then South Africa, the diplomatic and economic isolation of China . . .and the UN interventions in Bosnia and Somalia that began in 1992 in order to protect civilian populations... 'Human rights' has thus become an important legitimising icon that can allow interventions by one or more states in the internal affairs of others with relatively widespread global support. . . . . (Waters, 1995:103).

Concern for human rights is often the means by which international agendas—political and economic—are met. If it is convenient, and possible, for governments to intervene, or be seen to intervene, in order to win votes or look good, they will. But the profit/loss sum is calculated and the extent to which intervention occurs is frequently based on economic terms rather than the opportunity costs of not intervening.

Versions of Western capitalism are based on the "**individual greed is good** philosophy"; however, with the dictates of markets and challenge to "tighten our belts", the tendency for middle classes living in Western welfare states to blame "dole bludgers" has shifted to criticising the high wages of parliamentarians and managers of industry and the means by which profits are obtained. The idea that the middle classes will be content to be quiet citizen-consumers in their suburbs has changed. The "tightening of belts" philosophy under global capitalism has a very different result in this context.

The spill-over effects of the Asian economic crisis in 1998 have led toward revised attitudes to the way in which the state and business sectors operate. Social movements such as the student-lead movement in Indonesia have made a contribution to challenging the status quo.

In a changing socio-cultural, political, and economic climate, development practitioners, academics, and students need to develop long-term survival strategies as well as short-term pragmatism in order to maintain their ideals. "Both and thinking" is the order of the day. Social responses to complex problems of economics, social welfare, and the environment need to be holistic; human knowledge needs to be less discipline-based and more comprehensive. Competition and blame will be less relevant than collaboration and finding shared solutions. In a global context guided by the need to compete in world markets, cost cuts to welfare are also the order of the day. Those who first suffer the result of cutbacks are 'the other', who by virtue of gender, class position, age, race, culture, political affiliation, or physical or mental frailty are discriminated against. The other loser is the environment.

The world economic system or globalisation, according to Hettne (1995:121), ends the idea that we can think of development in isolation.

> Early development theory took for granted national development as a more or less automatic process and was concerned with the barriers to this process, rather than the mechanisms behind it. To

> some extent this bias has been overcome, but still it needs to be stressed that development is a differential result of human action, and that any development process consequently can be re-oriented through alternative human actions. As has been argued from a post-Marxist perspective (Corbridge 1990:634), it is important to return to radical development studies a sense of time and a sense of place. The imperative to take the global context into consideration does not change this. To get rid of the air of metaphysics and determinism that still surrounds the concept of development we could simply conceive it as societal problem solving, which would imply that a society as it succeeds in dealing with predicaments of a structural nature, many of them emerging from the global context... A major task is to analyse development predicaments stemming from the fact that most decision-makers operate in a national space but react on problems emerging in a global space over which they have only partial and often quite marginal control...." (Hettne 1995:263).

Hettne (1995) sums up his *Development Theory and the Three Worlds* with the conclusion that the positivist/formalist approaches to studying social reality have shifted as a result of critiques to include a normative/substantive approach. Instead of assuming that positivist research could lead to formal laws that can be generalised to many contexts, there is a realisation that development comprises a multiplicity of variables contextual in nature; unless the local cultural values are understood, development does not occur. He highlights the value of feminist, indigenous, and ecological models that give voice to marginalised women and colonised populations, and give particular recognition to the links amongst economics, social, and ecological structures. He also points out that in mainstream, conservative strands of development, the needs of the marginalised continue to be ignored (pp. 188,189). Generally, development approaches ignore the needs of the unemployed and those who cannot fulfill a productive role in the economy—

the homeless, mentally ill, young adolescents, law breakers, and ethnic groups who have been marginalised.

The notion that Western technology has all the answers has been shown to be very doubtful, even if capitalism is more pervasive than before. Pollution and poverty prevail in countries at both ends of the economic and ideological continuum of collectivism and individualism (Seabrook, 1990). The common denominators of both global options, as Weber (1978) pointed out, are bureaucracy and the cramping of creativity by the maintenance of vast administrative controls.

It is symptomatic of "either or thinking" to say that **modernisation** principles of development are *normative* and *controlling* and **postmodern** principles are *liberative*. Both paradigms hold positive and negative themes.

It is argued that reflexive thinking that weighs up the strengths and weaknesses of models within a particular environmental context is the vital skill required for democratic development. Teaching thinking tools can help sociological imagination. Giddens (1986:13) emphasised that the so-called "sociological imagination" espoused by C. Wright Mills (1975) can be aided by thinking in historical, anthropological, and critical terms.

Bearing this in mind: How can we think more creatively about problems? How can we manage/facilitate change? How can we structure social organisations? What kind of democracy do we want, what rights and what sorts of responsibility? To what extent can we argue that our common survival is interwoven and that we are bound to one another and our environment like Siamese twins?

One of the challenges in the postmodern, poststructural 1990s is to understand what democratic development means to all the people involved in life-style decisions, processes, and funding allocations. If we can move away from the idea that one ultimate meta-theory exists, we can move away from dogmatism. If we believe that social position, personality and emotion can shape perceptions, we can understand that some facts can be differently construed. If we wish to work with groups of people as global citizens, we need to have a sense of perceived 'private troubles' and how different interest groups translate these into 'public issues', to use the well-worn concepts of C. Wright Mills (1975). We need to keep in mind, however, that rational decisions balance individual diversity and rights with group responsibility to the ecosystem of which we are a small part.

Singer (1993) asks: How Are We to Live? He cites Alan Downing (1993:50) who asks: "can we equate consumption with fulfilment?" "The global economy now produces as much in seventeen days as the economy of our grandparents around the turn of the century produced in a year. . ." (Singer ,1993:42). All large economies whether they were based on capitalism or socialism, treated the environment as if extraction could be unending. The "unprecedented luxury that the upper and middle classes" (Singer, op. cit.) experience is at the cost of the poor and future generations. It is "living on our inheritance" (op cit.). For example, watering a golf course and gardens in an arid zone such as Alice Springs, Australia or privatizing water supplies is an approach which is neither humanistic nor ecological. It does not look closely at the long-term implications of policy on the environment and on those who will find it difficult to pay for water.

According to Giddens (1991) modernity is characterised by a sense of being out of touch with nature, because paradoxically nature is controlled to suit human needs. In recent times, the extremes of control (read exploitation) have led to a creation of unforeseen results and a creation of what Ulrich Beck (1992) called *Risk Society*.

We need to draw the connection between private troubles and choices and public issues and choices; we need to be aware that when we act locally, we have a global impact. Let us, for example, look at the fashion and automobile design industries. Both express artistic creativity common to all people; however, only wealthy nations inspire a sense of need through advertising seasonal fashion changes or tri-yearly automobile design changes that render wearable or "drivable" fashions of the previous seasons obsolete and confer a status position on those who continue to wear or drive them. Needs are created. Television programs watched in remote villages of less-developed countries inspire needs that remain unfulfilled. A sense of relative poverty compounds the experience of real poverty, where the most basic of human needs remain unmet. The time has come to consciously make the connections and strive to ensure that the voices of global citizens are joined in unison, so as to recognise shared goals and common concerns. Much can be learned about the necessity of living in harmony with nature: Water, soil, air, plants, animals, and human beings must co-exist harmoniously if the whole is to survive.

Citizens have the responsibility to understand the connections Singer (1993) spelled out across conspicuous consumption of luxury items and high protein diets, pollution, the greenhouse effect, the depletion of the ozone layer, the increase in cancers and plant and animal mutations as a result of increased exposure to harmful rays. He draws the connection across consumption of meat, deforestation, use of chemicals, and waste of resources. A taste for meat has led to overgrazing and degradation of fragile grazing lands. Choosing whether or not to eat meat is of wider relevance than we might originally understand. In Australia, the taste for beef and lamb has led to the destruction of indigenous fauna and flora and to a belated realisation that by introducing foreign species, the environmental balance has been disrupted. The rise in sea level is also connected with the greenhouse effect and could lead to the flooding of low-lying landmasses. Singer (p. 46) claims that Vanuatu, Tuvala and the Marshall Islands, for instance, could be completely lost. Similarly, he points out that choosing to drive a car to work every day and whether to use non-CFC-based products has an impact on pollution levels. We can, through consumer choices, help shift public opinion to taking personal responsibility away from creating greenhouse gases.

The choice to use a wide range of chemicals that are not biodegradable leads to some unexpected results. In ABC television documentary "Assault on the Male", made by the BBC, screened on October 24, 1996 in Australia, it was argued that modern chemicals are high in artificial oestrogen, and chemical wastes pumped into rivers have slowly had an impact on the reproductive organs of fish—male organs are undeveloped. U.S. and U.K. studies on wildlife showed an impact on the way fertility rates had reduced. Reducing the numbers and diversity of species will have ecological impacts that can be ascertained only through systemic thinking.

Singer (1993) outlines a history of capitalism, which is based on usury and the notion that money can earn money. Capitalism loses touch with the notion that toil reaps a limited reward. Instead, the notion that "greed is good" and a limitless environment can sustain limitless greed has backfired to a realisation that the environment is fragile and that we should be custodians of the environment rather than applying ongoing extraction. The ontological perspective of living in harmony versus living in opposition to the environment has both existential and epistemological implications concerning the nature of knowledge.

Social movements advocating new thinking need to be set up. It is an optimistic approach, because instead of assuming that structures are deterministic, there is faith in the human potential of groups of individuals to shape the societies in which they live through applying their creative potential. Thinking tools to help us map out the constructs of participants are vital for negotiation of meanings in order to restore social and environmental imbalances (Ife, 1995) and counterbalance the thinking strategies that privilege some voices and denigrate 'the other'. Denzin and Lincoln (1994) discuss the liberative potential of critical ethnography, narrative inquiry and feminist methodology. Importantly, Fine (in Denzin and Lincoln, 1994) stresses in her chapter "Working the Hyphens: Reinventing Self and Other in Qualitative Research", that researchers need to ensure that the voices of the other are not silenced by exploring the space between the 'self' and 'the other'. This means changing the existing balance of power at both the micro and macro levels. Negotiation requires an ability to read and record the constructs of stakeholders so that social action taken is perceived as appropriate by the have-nots and is likely to get as many of the haves on side as possible!

Any attempt at development work in the field of education needs to be 'disembedded', to use Giddens' term (Waters, 1995:49), from a purely local context, and the ramifications of causes and effects seen in broader terms. In what site should educational development take place? Should development take place in geographical space (within, for example, the neighbourhood, local council, state) or electronically generated acoustic, visual and geographical space created by groups with shared interests that wish to function together to achieve a particular aim? All problem-solving and development work needs to be placed within a wider context in order to understand the problem holistically in a multi-disciplinary and intersectoral manner, to use the terminology of the World Health Organisation's Ottawa Health Charter. According to Flood and Romm's (1996) language of systems thinking, we need to use a "total systems integration approach".

Essentially, Giddens is asking us to read the context and to allow the many voices from different readings to be heard. This is what paradigm dialogue (PD) is about. In order to be able to listen to others, we need tools to help us shift from uni-dimensional readings to multi-faceted readings. One of the ways we can hear the 'other' is by using revised forms of ethnographic techniques allowing researcher and researched to swap roles so that subject-to-subject dialogue can occur, rather than subject-to-object dialogue. Action research strives to 'learn by doing' together with others and, in the process, tries to find workable solutions that give the best *fit* to circumstances as far as stakeholders are concerned.

Giddens (1986:156) emphasised the continuities in meaning between the sociologist and his or her subject matter. The emic, or insider, knowledge of society and the etic, or outsider, knowledge are continuous, in so far as the social thinker sees what he/she perceives in terms of his/her own framework of meaning. Giddens uses these reflexive tools to address whether development leads to modern industrial states that will generate enough wealth for all, or whether capitalist development leads to transnational exploitation of local people and those in less-developed countries. He avers that in socialist and capitalist states, technology versus nature is not addressed—nor is the exploitation of people on the basis of race and gender. He also claims that "accumulation on a world scale" leads to global competition. Giddens who cites Amin (1988:150), claims furthermore that the role of the nation–state within global economies is competitive and violent.

7

Conclusion Beyond Nationalism: Striving for Global Democracy Within Conceptual Space, Cyberspace and Geographical Space

An Example of the Use of Dialogue to Forge Links at State Level in a New South Africa

The attempt by Bishop Desmond Tutu to use dialogue in South Africa as a way of re-making connections was high risk, because it leapt beyond the accepted parameters of the state that punishes criminals and rewards conformity. Bishop Tutu's conception of the use of dialogue for truth and reconciliation in Post-Apartheid South Africa attempted to create shared national identity and needs to be understood as an effort to co-create peace.

The state in South Africa prior to the end of Apartheid can be regarded as being the epitome of "power through conflict" versus "power through consensus". Concurrently, international changes to the welfare policy in most of the industrialised West away from universalism to residualism—in order to compete in global markets—has led to wide-ranging politically conservative and economic rationalist changes. Just when South Africa reached a stage when she was likely to be able to address the promises of the new electorate, the removal of tariff barriers became economic policy because the African National Congress (ANC) is determined that South Africa remain economically competitive in global markets. Balancing the needs of unemployed, unionised workers, and mobile global capital has become a challenge. Dealing with the pain of poverty and the lack of the most basic needs—housing, safe water, sanitation, and jobs—is a burden for the new electorate facing the challenges of global markets presented as imperatives that cannot be avoided.

The role of the Truth and Reconciliation Commission (TRC) needs to be considered as an exercise in paradigm dialogue, in so far as it tried to forge links of shared meaning and close spaces between the races created by Apartheid. Unfortunately, spaces created by class remain entrenched. There have been detractors to the Right and Left and criticisms—many quite justified—about the way in which the TRC has been used as a gravy train by some facilitators while others have escaped with murder. Far worse, torturers have appeared on Americanised South African TV talk shows flaunting their notoriety against a background of sleazy, sequined glitz. If this is shining the light on dark places, it is not what the TRC intended.

The TRC is worth holding up as an example of an attempt to move away from Aristotelian categories of right and wrong in order to try to forge a new beginning. The process has liberative potential because it attempts to demonstrate and prefigure growth through dialogue. It is a brave attempt against the nihilism of individualism, capitalism, and postmodernism, symbolised by the suggested conversion of the notorious state opera house in Preforia into a casino. Outside the opera house, where 'Art' was defined by the state and the status quo remained largely unchallenged due to censorship, Barend Strijdom massacred black people in Strijdom Square, so named after an Apartheid leader whose statue at that time presided over the space. He called himself 'White Wolf' and intimated that he represented 'Afrikanerdom'.

This drama was witnessed by many, including black street children who, at the time, were part of the Pretoria Street Wise Program for homeless children of which I was a founder. That night, they enacted a socio-drama of the event they had seen in order to exorcise the violence. One small child switched the drama from the horror of the White Wolf by becoming Superman and waving an imaginary cloak to rescue and revive the children who rolled around playing dead on the floor of the Salvation Army soup kitchen.

Tutu's attempt to introduce truth and reconciliation flies in the face of the shadowy postmodern notion that there is no truth and that our humanity is a meaningless gamble. Ubuntu is the belief that we are people through other people; it embraces both rights and responsibility. Traditional cosmology stresses that health—in the widest sense of the word—is only achievable if we are at one with ourselves, other people, and nature. Sitas (1998), amongst others, sounds the warning evident that the mantra of 'the rainbow nation' and pleas to 'Ubuntu' must be buttressed with real material improvements in living conditions. Reconciliation is easier for those who ride the gravy train of political jobs than for those whose children continue to die from gastroenteritis.

Dialogue is essential for a democracy. What can we, as global citizens, do to shift responsibility away from narrow individualism and nationalist self-interests on the one hand, and allowing the market to dictate, on the other hand? The multiple arenas in which we operate as citizens can no longer be restricted to the local. Instead, the space-time continuum has been broken down, and social action can occur through wide-ranging networks in cyberspace. Alliances can lead to social movements. But this *does not* mean there is no place for geographically located development work (Ife, 1995).

It is also true to say that social movements, called 'the new form of politics', are not only fluid responses by interest groups to complex challenges and social problems, they can be used to cut across bases for discrimination. These include: 1) demographic/biological bases: gender, age, racial origin, or phenotypical distinctions such as skin type or facial features; 2) sociocultural bases: religion or political grouping; and 3) economic cultural bases: wealth, status, and power.

According to Jennett and Stewart (1989:16) a common characteristic of so-called 'new social movements' is "to expand the area of control of the life world by the ordinary citizen. Although most aim to further their ends by having members elected to parliament, they all participate in direct action and civil disobedience of various sorts. . ."

They argue that since the late 1980s, the strategies have changed and quote as follows: "Touraine (1977) argues that the fundamental feature of postindustrial society is that transformative struggle must take place at the cultural level. This is in contrast to the view expressed by those old social movement activists and Marxist writers who see class struggle as the fundamental feature of social change." They go on to say that Touraine does not deny the importance of the class struggle, and associated politics activity.

Social movements can be understood in many different ways, depending on the sets of assumptions on which they are based. Those who see conflict only in class terms differ from Touraine, who sees a much wider basis for social movements because social controls have broadened beyond the economic to include the social and cultural domain (Touraine, 1995). However, Touraine does not deny class as an organising principle. According to Jennett and Stewart (1989:2–4):

> For Touraine, the social movements represent a profound cultural challenge and reflect disillusionment with the whole 'modernity project'. . .

> . . .[A] new social movement emerges when meta-social guarantees, such as modernity, are seen to be no longer relevant, and when change, or the study of social action, and the capacity of society to produce an historical experience through cultural patterns, is at the heart of social action. In other words, social movements must realise they are no longer limited by the old meta-social guarantees; they must begin to reflect in their social action the feeling we all have as individuals that our capacity for self-production, self - transformation and self-destruction is boundless (Touraine, 1985:778). In order to undertake transformation of the type characterised by Touraine, a social movement would have to engage in a battle for historicity, defined by Touraine (1977) as the creative work humans perform by inventing norms, institutions and practices to govern and make predictable their social relations . . . The charter of social movements is therefore the invention of new norms, institutions and practices. Social movements are not satisfied with structural change unless it is accompanied by a reformulation of historicity so as to generate new meaning, spirit and solidarity in the lives of individuals. Our contributors accept the definition of social movements as a form of collective action, made up of informal groups of people committed to broad change at the levels of individual behaviour, social institutions and structures".

The way in which we understand the world as social thinkers and citizens is shaped by our own lived experience. But by virtue of our shared humanity we have common denominators, and social movements are possible because of shared goals and can be normative in some respects.

Plurality of action can undermine the notion of class as an organising principle which can have advantages for ruling elites. If trade unionism is discarded entirely as an obsolete movement, it is to the advantage of economic rationalists and makes the worker without a cushion of wealth very vulnerable. Unionism **plus** other forms of social action should be considered. Once again, this is an example of the need for "both and thinking".

Also, although the state is no longer the most important base for organising social behaviour, it cannot be discarded as a unit of analysis. Multi-national companies and economic trading blocks are other important shapers of the life chances of individuals, which are usually mediated through the state whether it has contracted or expanded in response to global markets. The life chances of individuals are reflected in their cultural choices and consumer behaviour.

Socio-cultural, political, and economic contexts at micro and the macro levels are relevant for collaboration within geographical, acoustic, and visual space. Ife (1995:93) warns that cyberspace should never become an alternative for face-to-face community, but it can be a vital adjunct for lobbying on social and environmental issues globally. Small-scale action research projects can prefigure change at a wider level, provided the policy issues can be teased out and made available to a wider audience.

We need to use social movements to publicise and promote transcultural thinking tools so that people can create their own webs of meaning that can help link private troubles and public issues; the personal domain and public domain, the local neighbourhood with not merely the state public domain, but with international interest groups that span space and time. Social justice concerns are not the preserve of isolated groups if they can tap into wide-ranging networks. Social movements can respond in a fluid way to the needs of interest groups and, thereby, keep a vigilant watch on perceived infringements on democracy and help redress imbalances.

Touraine (1995) stresses that to be a subject, we need to engage in social movements and not accept that the market is rational or that it can or should dictate behaviour and thinking. The work of Stretton (1990) which emphasises that simplistic economic models do not capture the diversity of challenges facing modern economies, is a useful example of an alternative approach based on "both and thinking"—in so far as he advocates working with economic models and fine-tuning them to meet contextual variations. Keynesianism, re-visited and revised, could be an alternative approach according to this argument advocated by social movements (and trade unions) to act as a conscience, or a voice for the ordinary people.

The following survival strategies could be considered:

—To introduce young citizens at primary, secondary, and tertiary level to reflexive theory and methods to aid transcultural understanding and research in the global context. The work of Eva Cox in the 1995 Boyer lecture stressed "social capital". Citizenship rights and responsibility need to be highlighted in all educational contexts, as opposed to narrow economistic thinking that does not value people.

—To demonstrate an understanding of cultural constructs and idioms in all research and all problem-solving and to use technology for achieving sustainable development. This requires embracing the liberative potential of information technology, not denying its existence and retreating from all technology.

—To teach systemic thinking so that the weblike links across the socio-cultural, political, and economic contexts of researcher and researched are acknowledged.

—To use ecological thinking to solve social and environmental problems, rather than pitting the wild and natural environment against ordinary people and society. Environmental and social justice challenges need to be borne by both rich and poor nations, without shifting the blame and costs to poor nations. The social movements based on feminism and social justice issues and the various shades-of-green movements have developed with assumptions tied to particular life experience and could benefit from reflexive thinking. Top-down development, no matter how well-intended, cannot lead to long-term successes, unless all the stakeholders believe in a shared mission.

—To undertake Participatory Action Research (PAR) on global democracy to facilitate understanding of our common goals. Given the interconnections in our social and physical worlds, we can now think of a global community and ourselves as global citizens with rights and responsibilities that impact beyond our neighbourhood. In a world that is, on the one hand, shrinking in size through the creation of global networks, we continue to have parochial ideas based on categorising in terms of narrow frameworks informed by our own experiences rather than the experience of 'the other'. When we perceive that we are in some way threatened, we resort to creating barriers between insider and outsider. The rationalisation is that insiders have rights and outsiders are beyond the pale.

—Politicians should be required to analyse theories of race, gender, culture, poverty, class, and development and the way in which dominant paradigms portray, represent, and control 'the other'. The fear of the working class, beleaguered farmers, and the unemployed is that economic rationalism will continue to drive government decisions and those who are not central to the global economy will be forgotten. PAR is beneficial in creating links between the real world and the world of learning. It can also provide a valuable change opportunity for teaching and learning. Most importantly, it can provide the opportunity to make a real difference by prefiguring new ways of framing and addressing social issues. But, paradoxically, we should be mindful that PAR can be abused because, as a tool, it can create opportunities to exploit the people one is supposedly helping! This can occur when people are used as a means to an end, rather than as ends in themselves.

Development of social movements is about taking personal responsibility as global citizens. Giddens'(1991:214) notion of life politics, derived from the feminist aphorism "the personal is political", is a concept central to this construction of global citizenship. One such way this can be achieved is "through translating private troubles into public issues" to use C. Wright Mills phrase. By building leadership to address these public issues within the local, national, and international "community", a group of people with shared concerns can be created. Power is a relationship based on achieving integrations across interest groups.

Friedman (1992), in his book *Empowerment: The Politics of Alternative Development,* stressed that development was shaped within the domains of state and market, and in the private domains of household and local environment. As householders, people are able to shape the market and state as never before. This is because of information technology and also through making consumer choices within the marketplace or through boycotts and strikes within the production sphere. Whereas before we could conceptualise the state and market in terms of distinct national entities, now the state and market overlap. Most importantly, people are no longer necessarily just part of a mass society; they are able to engage in linking across time and space on the basis of shared interest. Never before has the potential for change through social movements been greater or, for that matter, more urgent. Individual citizens need to remain critical of the numbing effect of the mass media and to use the liberative potential of cyberspace to work in interest groups to ensure that human rights and environmental concerns remain at the forefront of political activity.

The separate nation-state has been transformed through wide-ranging socio-economic links into a mesh of overlapping interests. The change has a positive aspect, namely, the need to realise that nationalism is no longer appropriate. Global democracy emphasising our shared human, biological, and ecological interdependence is essential.

It is vital that discourses on democracy do not become diluted by merely concentrating on specific interest groups. We need to discover our common needs and use these common denominators as a vehicle for bringing about broad-based democracy, whilst acknowledging the diversity of our experience.

Despite the shortcomings of postmodernism discussed above, it has led to some humility in assuming that one model fits all circumstances. Post-structuralism has added even more to our understanding, insofar as emphasising that neat structural models sometimes do not capture the full complexity of a situation.

Global citizenship based on a shared sense of destiny needs to be fostered through social movements encouraging individuals and groups to use thinking tools to shift people away from thinking in adversarial terms of insider and outsider, in order to foster creativity through acknowledging diversity. Nationalist, sectarian, religious, political movements, and narrow trade unionism, which seeks to protect only the worker and not necessarily the environment and the unemployed, need to be replaced by multi-semic movements.

Every available opportunity for networking and social action needs to be pursued in a range of arenas: public (government and nongovernment organisations and committees), business, and the private sphere of citizens in their own homes—using their own modems, if they are privileged, and working to ensure that the disenfranchised are included in networks. Even if every household cannot be networked in poorer nations, a system of **old and new forms of communication should link rural and urban households** so that their concerns—separate and overlapping—could be included in regional discussions. The responsibility for addressing problems lies in a number of arenas, not the least of which is making capitalist corporations and consumers responsible for the intrinsic and extrinsic costs (Argyrous and Stilwell, 1996 ; and Daly and Cobb, 1994). If international law could regulate global markets so that company profits could never be built upon extracting surplus value from people and environments to their mutual detriment, this would be a first step toward achieving global democracy. The legal system should be revised to realise that law needs to reflect principles of justice to protect all people and the environment. By visualising a more just society and lobbying through social movements, this could occur.

The arenas are now fluid and can be created to suit the needs of a particular movement. Cyberspace and geographical space are sites for new social action to raise the conscience of groups of people. They must see that their future life chances are linked closely with one another and that global citizenship, which is *collaborative* and not *competitive,* is the order of the day. Leadership does not have to come from the powerful members of society. Leadership can come from principled individuals willing to take a stand and share insights gained through solving problems using thinking tools for inclusive, creative thinking, rather than trying to solve problems in terms of "either or thinking". The latter thinking so often lapses into racism or nationalism, or some other form of sectarian bigotry.

If we can build inclusive models premised on a belief in one environment and shared human needs then we can create a model that will include all costs (human and environmental) into a socially and environmentally sustainable model (Daly and Cobb, 1994). A sense of social responsibility can be taught, if we can be made aware through reflexive thinking that our futures are interlinked and our economic models need to build in social and environmental value not merely profit value to global markets.

This essay has attempted to provide some tools for global citizens who are concerned about the quality of their lives and the way in which their roles in private and public life could be enhanced by working for creative solutions through wide ranging social movements, **to achieve social contracts through paradigm dialogue,** rather than solutions merely in their own interests.

Legal systems have operated according to binary oppositional logic. The notion of ownership does not have to be "either or" but can be "both and". The sharing of land is possible if it is used in a sustainable way. The struggle for land in many parts of the world between first nations and colonists continues, and solutions are possible if "both and thinking" prevails. All problem-solving and development work needs: 1)to be 'disembedded', to use Giddens' term; 2) placed within a wider context, in order to understand the problem holistically in a multi-disciplinary and intersectoral manner, to use the terminology of the World Health Organisation's Ottawa Health Charter; or 3) in Flood and Romm's (1996) language, to use a "Total Systems Integration approach". The extraction of so-called 'surplus value' from humans and the environment has a cost to both. Only systems, as opposed to categorical thinking, can help us understand the complexity of problems and address them. An integrated approach to understanding the world could lead to improved social measures to promote social health and prevent problems from occurring.

End Notes

1. ABS National Aboriginal and Torres Strait Islander Survey, 1997. The NT Government Health Policy , NT Website on Public Health Northern Territory Health Outcomes-Morbidity and Mortality 1979-1991 quoted in Public Health NT website. Australian Bureau of Statistics (1997) The Health and welfare of Australia's Aboriginal and Torres Strait Islander Peoples Report NO 4704.0.
2. Tangentyere Council Annual Report 1997-98, page 23.
3. See "Women's citizens' struggle for citizenship" by Weeks,W. in The Australian Welfare State Democratic leadership practices in Australian feminist Women's Services : the pursuit of Collectivity and Social Citizenship? In International review of Women and Leadership (1996) 2 (1) 19-33
4. Reflective approaches in counselling aim to demonstrate an empathy and mutual understanding with the other.
5. Office of Women's Policy, Northern Territory Government. 1996. Domestic Violence Strategy: The Financial and Economic Costs of Domestic Violence.
6. According to Jane Vadiveloo, spokesperson for the Youth at Risk Committee set up earlier in 1998 in response to the spate of suicides in an article in the Alice Springs News 5 (43): 25 November 1998 entitled "Care or cane? Suicides raise big questions!", the issue of using a punishment versus a caring and preventative approach was raised. The Northern Territory has an imprisonment rate three times higher than Western Australia. "The number of prisoners per 100,000 population, according to Mr Stirling, is Act 60.6, Victoria 70.6, Tasmania 75.6, South Australia 128.5, NSW 132.6,

WA 165, NT 459.3." Mr Stirling says "Under mandatory sentencing this figure will continue to increase because every young person imprisoned is four times more likely to appear before the courts again compared to those detained".

"Mr Stirling says under mandatory sentencing the daily average number of Territorians in prison has grown to 610 during 1997-98 compared in the preceding year".

Bibliography

Aarons, A. 1983 . Teachers and health workers: Partners in PHC. *Community Development Journal* 18(2):32–38.

Ackroyd, C., and J. Hughes. 1992. *Data Collection in Context.* London:Longman.

Argyrous, G., and F. Stilwell, eds. 1996. *Economics as a Social Science: Readings in Political Economy.* Marrickville:Pluto Press.

Alinsky, S. D. 1972. *Rules for Radicals: A Practical Primer for Realistic Radicals.* New York: Vintage.

Armstrong, J., and P. Henderson 1992. Putting the community into community care. *Community Development Journal* 27(2):189–192.

Ashton, J. et al. 1986. Healthy cities—WHO's new public health initiative. *Health Promotion* 1(3).

Bales, R. F. 1958. Task roles and social roles in problem-solving groups. In Maccoby et al., *Readings in Social Psychology,* Third edition New York: Holt, Rinehart and Winston.

Baron, R. A. 1986. *Behavior in Organisations: Understanding and Managing the Human Side of Work.* Second edition. Boston: Allyn & Bacon.

Baum, F. et al. 1990 July. *Healthy cities: Noarlunga evaluation. Southern Community Health Research Unit,* South Australia Health Commission.

Bateson, G. 1972. *Steps to an Ecology of Mind: A Revolutionary Approach to Man's Understanding of Himself.* New York: Ballantine.

Beer, S. 1974. *Designing Freedom.* London: Wiley.

Beck, U. 1992. *Risk Society: Towards a New Modernity.* London: Sage.

Beilharz, P. 1993. Sociology strikes back: The impact of economic rationalism in Canberra. *The Australian and New Zealand Journal of Sociology* 29 (3):369–273.

Beilharz, P., M. Considine, and R. Watts. 1992 *Arguing About the Welfare State: the Australian Experience.* Sydney: Allen and Unwin.

Bell, C., and H. Newby. 1971. *Community Studies: An Introduction to the Sociology of the Local Community.* Sydney: Allen and Unwin.

Bell, D. 1983. *Daughters of the Dreaming.* Sydney: Allen and Unwin.

——. 1993. *Communitarianism and Its Critics.* Oxford: Clarendon .

Bell, S. 1993. Weak on the State: Economic Rationalism in Canberra. *The Australian and New Zealand Journal of Sociology* 29(3):387–401.

Berger, P. 1976. *Pyramids of Sacrifice: Political Ethics and Social Change.* Harmondsworth: Penguin.

Berger, P. L. 1977. *Facing Up to Modernity.* Harmondsworth, Penguin.

——. 1997. *Redeeming Laughter: The Comic Dimension of Human Experience.* Walter De Gruyter.

Berger, P. L., and Luckmann. 1967. *The Social Construction of Reality: A Treatise on the Sociology of Knowledge.* Anchor.

Berger, P., B. Berger, and K. Heinsfield. 1974. *The Homeless Mind: Modernization and Consciousness.* Harmondsworth: Penguin.

Blaikie, N. 1993. *Approaches to Social Enquiry.* Cambridge: Polity.

——. 1998. A parable of four paradigms. *14th World Congress of Sociology.* Montreal.

Boeren, A. 1992. Getting involved: communication for participatory development. *Community Development Journal.* 27(3):259–271.

Boonzaier, E., and J. Sharp. 1988. *South African Keywords: The Uses and Abuses of Political Concepts.* Cape Town: David Philip.

Borman G. E. 1990. *Small Group Communication: Theory and Practice.* New York: Harper and Row.

Bowden, M. 1994. *Will There Be Aboriginals as We Are Today: A Case Study of the Education of Arrernte Youth in Alic Springs.* Master thesis submitted in partial fulfillment of the requirements for the degree of Master of Education at the Northern Territory University.

Bourdieu, P. 1987. *In Other Words: Essays Towards a Reflexive Sociology.* Sage: London.

Bourdieu, P., and L. J. D. Wacquant. 1992. *An Invitation to Reflexive Sociology.* Cambridge: Polity.

Boyers, R., and R. Orril. 1972. *Laing and Anti-Psychiatry.* Penguin.

Brager, G., and H. Specht. 1975. The process of community work. In *Readings in Community Organisation Practice,* (second edition). Englewood, Cliffs, New Jersey: Prentice Hall.

Braithwaite, J. 1993. Beyond positivism: Learning from contextual integrated strategies. *Journal of Research in Crime and Delinquency* 30 (4):3383–3399.

——. 1998. *Crime, Shame and Reintegration.* Melbourne: Cambridge University Press.

Brauer, T. 1996. What would you expect of a boy named Sue? *Systems Practice* 9(4):357–376.

Braverman, H. 1974. *Labor and Monopoly Capital: The Degradation of Work in the Twentieth Century.* New York: Monthly Review Press.

Bryson, L. 1992. *Welfare and the State: Who Benefits?* London: Macmillan.

Bryson, L., and M. Mowbray. 1981. Community: The spray-on solution. *Australian Journal of Social Issues* 16(4):255–266.

Buber, M. 1965. *Between Man and Man.* New York: Macmillan.

Bulbeck, C. 1993. *Social Sciences in Australia.* Sydney: Harcourt Brace.

Bulmer, M. 1987. *The Social Basis for Community Care.* London: Allen and Unwin.

Burgman, V. 1993. *Power and Protest: Movements for Change in Australian Society.* Sydney: Allen and Unwin.

Burkett, I. 1996. Educating for community work practice in a globalising world. Paper presented at the AASWWE Conference. 1–4 October. University of Melbourne, Victoria.

Cadbury, D. 1997. *The Feminization of Nature: Our Future at Risk.* London: Hamish Hamilton.

Camilleri, J., and J. Falk. 1992. *The End of Sovereignty: The Politics of a Shrinking and Fragmenting World.* Aldershot: Edward Elgar.

Castells, M. 1996. *The Rise of Network Society.* Oxford: Blackwell.

——. 1997. *The Power of Identity.* Oxford: Blackwell.

——. 1996–1998. *The Information Age: Economy, Society and Culture.* Malden Mass: Blackwell.

Chambers, R. 1983. *Rural Development: Putting the Last First.* New York: Wiley.

Chambers, I. 1990. *Border Dialogues: Journeys into Postmodernity.* London: Routlege.

Chomsky, N. 1993. *Year 501: The Conquest Continues.* London: Verso.

Colinvaux, P. 1978. *Why Big Fierce Animals Are Rare.* Princetown University Press.

Colinvaux, P. 1980. *The Fates of Nations: A Biological Theory of History.* New York: Simon and Schuster.

——. 1986. *Ecology.* New York: Wiley.

Cooper, L. 1992. What about incompetent practice? Paper delivered at the National Conference on *The Challenge of Competencies in Social Welfare.* Adelaide, South Australia.

Corbin, J. and A. Strauss. 1990. *Basics of Qualitative Research: Grounded Theory Procedures and Techniques.* London: Sage.

Corbridge, S. 1986. *Capitalist World Development: A Critique of Radical Development Geography. London*: Frank Cass.

Coulehan, K. 1998. *Alice Springs: a cultural crossroads and a service and transit centre for Aboriginal people in Central Australia.*Cox, F., Erlich, J,Rothman, J and Tropman, E. (1979) Strategies of community organization. Itasca, Illonois. Peacock.

Cox, E. 1995. *A Truly Civil Society.* Sydney NSW, ABC Books. Boyer Lectures.

Cox. F., J. Erlich, J. Rothman, and E. Tropman. 1979. *Strategies of Community Organization.* Itasca, Illinois: Peacock.

Crane, J., and M. Angrosino. Field. 1974. *Projects in Anthropology: A Student Handbook.* New Jersey: General Learning Press.

Crick, M., and Geddes 1993. *Research Methods in the Field: Ten Anthropological Accounts.* Geelong: Deakin University Press.

Crook, S., J. Pakulski, and M. Waters. 1993. *Postmodernisation.* London: Sage.

Daly, H. and J. Cobb. 1994. *For the Common Good.* Boston: Beacon.

Dana, D. 1990. *Talk It Out: Four Steps to Managing People Problems in Your Organization.* London: Kegan Page.

Davidson, A.I . 1997. *Foucault and His Interlocutors.* London: University of Chicago Press.

Davies, J., and M. Kelly. 1993. *Healthy Cities: Research and Practice.* London: Routledge.

De Bono, E. 1977. *The Happiness Purpose.* Penguin.

——. 1993. *Water Logic: The Alternative to I Am Right and You Are Wrong.* England: Penguin.

Denzin, N., and Y. Lincoln. 1994. *Handbook of Qualitative Research.* London: Sage.

Dey, I. 1993. *Qualitative Data Analysis: A User Friendly Guide for Social Scientists.* London: Routledge.

Doel,M., and S. Shardlow. 1996. *Social Work in a Changing World: An International Perspective on Practice Learning.* Aldershot: Ashgate.

Donovan, F., and A. C. Jackson. 1991. *Managing Human Service Organizations.* Sydney:Prentice-Hall.

Downie, R. S., and E. Telfer. 1971. *Respect for Persons: A Philosophical Analysis of the Moral, Political and Religious Idea of the Supreme Worth of the Individual Person.* London: Allen and Unwin.

Elsey, B., and J. McIntyre. 1996. Assessing a support and learning network for palliative care workers in a country area of South Australia Australian. *Journal of Rural Health* 4:159–164.

Emmett, A. 1984. Theories of development. Occasional Paper. Human Sciences Research Council: Pretoria, South Africa.

Ernst, J., and L. Glanville. 1995. From citizens to customers: The impact of compulsory competitive tendering on the organisation and function of local government in Victoria. *Australian Association News Letter* (September).

Erskine, J. M. 1985. Rural development: putting theory into practice. *Development Southern Africa* 2(2): 368–383.

Fals-Borda, O., and M. A. Rahman. 1991. *Action and Knowledge: Breaking the Monopoly with Participatory Action Research.* London: Intermediate Technology.

Fetterman, D. 1989. *Ethnography Step By Step.* London: Sage.

Feuerstein, M. T. 1986. *Partners in Evaluation.* London: Macmillan.

Fine, M. 1994. Working the Hyphens: Reinventing Self and Other in Aualitative Research in *Handbook of Qualitative Research.* Norman K. Denzin, Y. S. Lincoln. Handbook of Qualitative Research. London: Sage.

Fisher, R., and W. Ury. 1991. *Getting to Yes: Negotiating Agreement Without Giving In.* Boston: Mifflin.

Flood, R. 1998. Action research and the management and systems sciences. *Systems Practice and Action Research* 11(1).

Flood, R., and N. Romm. 1996. *Diversity Management: Triple Loop Learning.* Chichester: Wiley.

Fonow, M., and J. Cook. 1991. *Beyond Methodology: Feminist Scholarship as Lived Research.* Bloomington: Indiana University Press.

Foucault, M. 1967. *Madness and civilization: A History of Insanity in the Age of Reason.* London: Routlege.

Foucault, M. and C. Gordan. ed. 1980, *Power/Knowledge: Selected Interviews and Other Writings 1972- 1977.* Brighton: Harvester.

Fox, E. and L. Urwick. 1973. *Dynamic Administration: The Collected Papers of Mary Parker Follett.* London: Pittman.

Freire, P. 1982. Creating alternative research methods: Learning to do it, in Hall, B., Gillette, A. and Tandon, R. Creating Knowledge: a monopoly? Society for participatory research in Asia, New Delhi: 29-37 in The Action Research Reader, Deakin University publication.

Frey, J. and A. Fontana. 1993. Interviewing: The art of science. In *A source Book of Qualitative Research Methods*, ed. N. Denzin and Y. Lincoln. London: Sage.

Friedman, J. 1992. *Empowerment: The Politics of Alternative Development.* Oxford: Blackwell.

Fukuyama, F. 1992. *The End of History and the Last Man.* London: Hamish Hamilton.

Game, A. and Metcalfe 1996. *Passionate Sociology.* London: Sage.

Gastill, J. 1993. *Democracy in Small Groups.* New Society.

Geddes, B., J. Hughes, and J. Remenyi. 1994. *Anthropology and Third World Development.* Victoria, Deakin University Press.

Geertz, C. 1973. Thick description: Towards an interpretive theory of culture. In *The Interpretation of Cultures. Selected Essays,* ed. C. Geertz, 3–32. New York: Basic.

Giddens, A. 1984. The Constitution of Society: Outline of the Theory of Structuration. Oxford: Polity.

——. 1986. *Sociology: A Brief but Critical Introduction.* London: Macmillan.

——. 1991. *Modernity and Self-Identity: Self and Society in the Late Modern Age.* Stanford: California.

——. 1995. *A Contemporary Critique of Historical Materialism.* London: Macmillan.

Gilligan, C. 1982. *In a Different Voice: Psychological Theory and Women's Development.* Cambridge: Harvard University Press.

Gouldner, A.W. 1971. *The Coming Crisis of Western Sociology.* London: Heinemann.

——. 1980. *The Two Marxisms: Contradictions and Anomalies in the Development of Theory.* London: Macmillan.

Graham, P. 1991. *Integrative Management: Creating Unity from Diversity.* USA: Basil Blackwell.

Graycar, A., and A. Jamrozik. 1989. *How Australians Live: Social Policy in Theory and Practice.* Melbourne: Macmillan.

Groenewald, J. P. 1986. *Social Research: Design and Analysis.* Grahamstown: University Publishers.

Goldthorpe, J. H., D. Lockwood, F. Bechhofer. and J. Platt. 1968. *The Affluent Worker in the Class Structure.* Cambridge: Cambridge University Press.

Grossberg, L., C. Nelson, P. Treichler. 1992. *Cultural Studies*. London: Routledge.

Grundy, S. 1982. Three modes of action research, Curriculum Perspectives, In *The Action Research Reader,* 2(3):23–34 Melbourne: Deakin University Press.

Guba, E., and Y. Lincoln. 1989. *Fourth Generation Evaluation*. London: Sage.

Habermas, J. 1974. *Theory and Practice.* London: Heinemann.

Hakim, C. 1987. *Research Design: Strategies and Choices in the Design of Social Research.* London: Allen and Unwin.

Haralambos, M. 1985. *Sociology: Themes and Perspectives.* London: Bell and Hyman.

Harker, R. and C. Mahar, and C. Wilkes. 1990. *An Introduction to the Work of Pierre Bourdieu: The Practice of Theory.* London: Macmillan.

Henderson, P., and D. Thomas. 1980. *Skills in Neighbourhood Work.* London: Allen and Unwin.

Hersey, P., and K. Blanchard. 1988. *Management of Organisational Behaviour: Utilising Human Resources.* London: Prentice Hall.

Herzberg, F. 1975. 'One more time': How do you motivate employees? In *Harvard Business Review, On Management*. New York: Harper and Row.

Hettne, B. 1995. *Development Theory and the Three Worlds: Towards an International Political Economy of Development*. England: Longman.

Hewitt, T., H. Johnson, and D. Wield. 1992. *Industrialization and Development*. Oxford: Oxford University Press.

Hil, R. 1994. Changing targets? Queensland's approach to crime prevention revisited. *Criminology Australia* 5(3):17–19.

Homant, R. and Osowski. 1981. Evaluation of the 'scared straight' model: some methodological and political considerations. *Journal of Behaviour Technology Methods and Therapy* 27(33):130–134.

Hughes, J. 1990. *The Philosophy of Social Research*. Essex: Longman.

Ife, J. 1995. *Community Development: Creating alternatives-Vision, Analysis and Practice*. Melbourne: Longman.

——. 1996. *Rethinking Social Work—Towards Critical Practice*. Melbourne: Longman.

Illich, I. 1978. *The Right to Useful Unemployment and Its Professional Enemies*. Open University Series. London.

Jackson, T., S. Mitchell, and M. Wright. 1989. *The Community Development Continuum in Community Health Studies*. 13(1):66–73.

Jamrozik, A., and L. Nocella. 1998. *The Sociology of Social Problems: Theoretical Perspectives and Methods of Intervention*. Cambridge: Cambridge University Press.

Janzen, J. 1978. *Quest for Therapy in Lower Zaire*. Berkeley: University of California Press.

Jennett, C., R. Stewart. 1989. *Politics of the Future: The Role of Social Movements*. Melbourne: Macmillan.

Johnson, P. 1994. *Feminism as Radical Humanism*. Allen and Unwin.

Johnson, D., and F. Johnson. 1987. *Joining Together*. Sydney: Prentice Hall.

Jones, A. 1992. Community development training—a comparative approach. *Community Development Journal* 27(3):199–210.

Jones, B. 1990. *Sleepers Wake! Technology and the Future of Work*. Third edition. Melbourne: Oxford University Press.

Kalantzis, M. 1992. Competencies, credentials and cultures. *Education Australia* 18:5–7.

Kaplan and Ziegler 1985. Class, hierarchies andsocial control. In *Human Organization*. 44.

Karpin, D. 1994. Address on leadership and management skills delivered to the Committee for the Economic Development of Australia. Melbourne.

Keene, I. 1988. *Being Black: Aboriginal Cultures in 'Settled' Australia*. Canberra: Aboriginal Press.

Keesing, R. M. 1987. Anthropology as interpretive quest. *Current Anthropology* 28(2):161–176.

Kelly, A. and S. Sewell. 1988. With Head and Heart and Hand: Dimensions in Community Building. Brisbane: Boolarong.

Kenny, S. 1994. *Developing Communities for the Future*. Melbourne: Nelson.

Kettner, P., J. Daley, and A. Nichols. 1985. *Initiating Change in Organizations and Communities*. Monterey: Brooks/Cole.

Korten, D. 1995. *When Corporations Rule the World*. London: Earthscan.

Krugman, P. 1994. *The Age of Diminished Expectations*. Third edition, reprinted in 1997. London: MIT Press.

Kuhn, T. 1970. *The Structure of Scientific Revolutions*. Chicago: University of Chicago Press.

Lackey, A. S., and Dershem 1992. The process is pedagogy: what does community participation teach? *Community Development Journal* 27(3):220–234.

Laing, R. D. 1960. *The Divided Self*. London: Tavistock. 1965. Penguin.

Langan and Day 1992. *Women, Oppression and Social Work*. London: Routlege.

Larrabee M. J. 1993. *An Ethic of Care: Feminist and Interdisciplinary Perspectives*. London: Routlege.

Levy Strauss, C. 1987. *Anthropology and Myth Lectures*. 1951–1982. Oxford: Blackwell.

Lewin, K. 1946. Action research and minority problems. *Journal of Social Issues* 2(4):34–46.

Lleras, E. 1996. Is it possible to develop an emancipatory approach to technology? *Systems Practice.* 9(4):333–338.

Marshall, C. 1995. *Designing Qualitative Research.* London: Sage.

Marshall, T. H. 1977. *Class, Citizenship and Social Development.* Chicago: University of Chicago Press.

Maslow, A. 1954. *Motivation and Personality.* New York: Harper and Row.

Maturana, H., and F. Verela. 1973. *Autopoiesis: The Organisation of Living.* Boston: Reidel.

——. 1980. *Autopoiesis and Cognition: The Realisation of Living.* Boston: Reidel.

Mayer, E. 1992. Mayer Committee: Employment-related key competencies: a proposal for consultation. Australian Educational Council and Ministers for Vocational Education, Employment and Training. Melbourne.

Mayo, E. 1945. *The Social Problems of an Industrial Civilisation.* Boston: Harvard Business School.

McCann, M. 1992. Epistemic games, transfer, and the six party hats: What the world's great thinkers are thinking. 5th International Conference on Thinking: Exploring Human Potential. *The Australian Journal of Gifted Education.* James Cook University. 1(2)

McClung L. A. 1988. *Sociology for People: Toward a Caring Profession.* New York: Syracuse University Press.

McIntyre, J. 1995. *Achieving Social Rights and Responsibility: Towards a Critical Hhumanist Approach to Community Development.* Community Quarterly Book. Melbourne.

——. 1996. Tools for Ethical Thinking and Caring: A Reflexive Approach to Theory and Practice in the Pragmatic 90's. Melbourne: Community Quarterly Book.

——. 1998. Paradigm dialogue: tools for ethical thinking and caring. Panel contribution in Methodology Group. 14th World Congress of Sociology, Montreal.

——. 1998. Consideration of categories and tools for holistic thinking. *Systemic Practice and Action Research.* 11(2).

McKay, V., and N. Romm. 1992. People's Education in Theoretical Perspective: Towards the Development of a Critical Humanist Approach. Cape Town: Maskew Miller Longman.

McKeown, T. 1965. *Medicine in mModern Society.* London: Allen and Unwin.

McLachlan, G., and T. Mckeowan. 1971. *Medical History and Medical Care: A Symposium of Perspectives.* Oxford: Oxford University Press

McLuhan, M., and B. Powers. 1989. *The Global Village: Transformations in World Life in the 21st Century.* Oxford: Oxford University Press.

McTaggart, R., and Garbutcheon-Singh. 1988. A fourth generation of action research :Notes on the Deakin Seminar. In *The Action Research Reader.* Victoria: Deakin University Press.

Mead, G. 1995. A Royal Commission: a critical summary of the evidence given to the Hindmarsh Island Bridge Royal Commission with an alternative report. South Australia.

Mead, G. H. 1974. *Mind, Self and Society.* Chicago: University of Chicago Press.

Meekosha, H. Anger and angst: Responding to hate, conflict and violence in the Australian Community. *Community Development Journal* 29(2):158–168.

Meekosha, H., and M. Mowbray. 1990. Reconstruction to deconstruction: The transformation of community work in Australia. *The Community Development Journal* 25(4).

Mensies, G. 1992. The challenge of competencies in social welfare. Paper delivered at the *National Conference on the Challenge of Competencies in Social Welfare.* University of South Australia, Adelaide.

Miles, M. B., and A. M. Huberman. *Qualitative Data Analysis: A Sourcebook of New Methods.* London: Sage.

Mills, C. W. 1975. *The Sociological Imagination*. Harmondsworth: Penguin.

Mills, J. J. 1983. Health, healing and disease in a South African township. Unpublished M.A thesis. Department of Social Anthropology, University of Cape Town, South Africa.

——. 1985. Intwaso, an anthropological re-appraisal. *Journal of South African Sociology*. 16(1):9–13.

——. 1986. A pilot study to assess rural water supplies and sanitation conditions on the Pongolo Floodplain: A social anthropological perspective. *Development Southern Africa* 3(3):479–499.

——. 1987a. Diviners as social healers. *Journal of South African Sociology* 18(1):7–13.

——. 1987b. A sociological study of water and sanitation-related diseases as a sociopolitical phenomenon in South Africa. Unpublished D. Lit et Phil thesis. Department of Sociology, University of South Africa.

——. 1990a. Rural fieldwork in rural Boschfontein, KaNgwane: retrospective insights. *In Truth be in the Field : Social Science research in Southern Africa*. ed. P. Hugo, Pretoria: University of South Africa.

——. 1990b. From negotiation to bargaining: A sociological enquiry. In *Sociology and Society: A Humanistic Profile*, ed. C. Alant, Pretoria: University of South Africa.

Mingers, J. 1995. *Self-Producing Systems: Implications and Applications of Autopoiesis*. London: Plenum.

Moss-Kanter, R. 1989. Becoming PALS: Pooling, Allying, and Linking across Companies. *The Academy of Management Executive*. 3(3):183–193.

Moss-Kanter, R. 1991. Transcending business boundaries : 12,000 world managers view change. *Harvard Business Review* (May-June):151-164 .

Nobuko, I. 1998. Environmental deterioration and interrelationship between global and local inequalities: Perspectives from Asia and Australia. 14th World Congress of Sociology, Montreal.

Onyx, J., P. Benton, and J. Bradfield. 1992. Community development and government response. *Community Development Journal* 27(2): 166–174.

Perry, J., and J. Hughes. 1995. *Anthropology: Voices from the Margins.* Deakin University Press: Geelong.

Pixley, J. 1993. *Citizenship and Employment: Investigating Post-Industrial Options.* Melbourne: Cambridge.

Polanyi, M. 1962. *Personal Knowledge.* London: Routledge and Kegan Paul.

Popper, K. 1968. *The Logic of Scientific Discovery.* London: Hutchinson.

Quine, W. V., and J. S. Ullian. 1970. *The Web of Belief.* Random House.

Ragg, N. 1977. *People Not Cases: A Philosophical Approach to Social Work.* London: Routlege.

Reason, P. 1988. *Human Inquiry in Action.* London: Sage.

Reason, P. 1991. Power and conflict in multidisciplinary collaboration. *Complementary Medical Research.* 5(3) .

Rees, S. 1991. *Achieving Power: Practice and Policy in Social Welfare.* Sydney: Allen and Unwin.

Romm, N. 1991. Epistemological debates in Marxism. Paper delivered at the 22nd Annual Conference of the Association for Sociology in Southern Africa, University of Cape Town.

Romm, N. 1996. Inquiry and intervention in systems planning: Probing methodological rationalities. *World Futures* 47:25–36.

Romm, N. 1998. The process of validity checking through paradigm dialogues. 14th World Congress of Sociology, Montreal.

Romm, R. A. 1991. *The Methodologies of Positivism and Marxism: A Sociological Debate.* London: Macmillan.

Romm, N., and F. Holscher. 1986. Development as process of human consciousness: elements of a humanist view on development. In Development Is for People. ed. J. K. Coetzee, Johannesburg: Macmillan.

Rosaldo, R. 1993. Culture and Truth: The Remaking of Social Analysis. London: Routlege.

Rothman, J. 1979. Three models of community organisation. In *Strategies of Community Organisation*, ed. F. M. Cox, et al., Third edition. Itasca, Illinois: Peacock.

Salmon, W. 1973. *Logic Foundations of Philosophy.* Englewood Cliffs, New Jersey: series Prentice-Hall.

Sandercock, L. 1986. Economy versus Community, *Australian Society*:12–15.

Sarantakos, S. 1993. *Social Research.* Melbourne: Macmillan.

Saunders, P. and D. Encel. 1992. Social policy in Australia: Options for the 1990's. Proceedings of National Social Policy Conference. Sydney, 3–5 July 1991. Contributed papers, SPRC reports and proceedings. Vol. 3. Social Policy Research Centre, No. 98 (February). University of New South Wales.

Scott, J. 1991. *Social Network Analysis: A Handbook.* London: Sage.

Seabrook, J. 1988. *The Race for Riches: The Human Cost of Wealth.* Basingstoke: Green.

Seabrook, J. 1990. *The Myth of the Market: Promises and Illusions.* Devon: Green.

Shannon, S. 1993. Dilemmas of feminist ethnography. *The Discursive Construction of Knowledge: A Conference,* Adelaide University.

Singer, P. 1993. *How Are We To Live: Ethics in an Age of Self-Interest?* Melbourne: Text publishing.

Sitas, A. 1998. Beyond Afro pessimism. Identity and development in a globalising world. In *Gathering voices: Perspectives on the Social Sciences in Southern Africa.* ISA pre-Congress volumes .

Smaling, A. 1998). The paradigm dialogue: what kind of dialogue should it be? 14th World Congress of Sociology, Montreal.

Smith, S., and S. Williams. 1992. Remaking the connections. *Health Worker Journal,* 16(16).

Stacey, D. 1997. *Remaking Men: The Revolution in Masculinity.* Viking

Stanley, L. and S. Wise. 1993. *Breaking Out Again: Feminat Ontology and Epistemology.* London: Routlege.

Streeten, 1984. Basic needs: Some unsettled questions. Carnegie Conference Paper, No. 8: Cape Town.

Strehlow, T. G. H. 1978. *Central Australian Religion.* Australian Association for the Study of Religions. Adelaide: Flinders University.

Stretton, H. 1990. Australia on the road to Mexico. Unpublished. Longer version published under a different title in the first issue of Australian Options.

South Australian Health Commission, 1990. A Social Health Atlas of South Australia. SA Health Commission Publication.

Thurow, L. 1996. *The Future of Capitalism: How Today's Economic Forces Will Shape Tomorrow's World.* New York: Allen and Unwin.

Toffler, A. 1990. *Power Shift.* New York: Bantam.

Tomlinson, J. 1996. Citizenship and sovereignty. *Australian Journal of Social Science* 31(1).

Touraine, A. 1995. *Critique of Modernity.* Oxford: Blackwell.

Turner, B. S. 1993. *Citizenship and Social Theory.* London: Sage.

Twelvetrees, A. 1991. *Community Work.* Second edition. London: Macmillan.

Tyson, T. 1989. *Working with Groups.* Melbourne: Macmillan.

United Nations. 1991. *The World's Women: Trends and Statistics 1970–1990.*

Utke, A. R. 1986. The cosmic holism concept: An interdisciplinary tool in the quest for ultimate reality and meaning. *Ultimate Reality and Meaning.* 9:134–155.

Van Gennep. 1960. *Rites de Passage.* London: Routledge and Kegan Paul.

Van Gigch, J. P. 1997. The design of an epistemology for the management discipline which resolves dilemmas among ethical and other imperatives. *Systems Practice* 10(4).

Vecchiho, R. P., G. Hearn, and G. Southey. 1988. *Organisational Behaviour: Life and Work in Australia.* Sydney: Harcourt Brace.

Vellekoop-Baldock, C. 1990. *Volunteers in Welfare.* Sydney: Allen and Unwin.

Waters, M. 1995. *Globalization.* London: Routlege.

Weber, M. 1978. *Economy and Society.* Berkeley: University of California Press.

Weeks, W. 1996. Women's struggle for citizenship. In *The Australian Welfare State,* ed. J. Wilson, J. Thomson, and A. McMahon. Melbourne: Macmillan.

Weizenbaum, J. 1976. *Computer Power and Human Reason: From Judgement to Calculation.* San Francisco: Freeman.

Weil, S. 1998. Reflexive turns in paradigm dialogues; tensions and challenges in transcending different domains for knowledge generation. 14th World Congress of Sociology, Montreal.

Werlin, H. 1989. The community: Master or client?—A review of the literature. *Public Administration and Development* 9:447–457.

White, R., and C. Alder. 1994. *The Police and Young People in Australia.* Cambridge: Cambridge University Press.

Wilhelmij, P., A. Holden, B. Reynolds, and B. Liew. 1995. Life track: Enhancing team knowledge and corporate memory in petrochemical operations through sharing lessons learned. Paper delivered at Safety-Critical Systems Conference. Leeds, United Kingdom.

Wilson, J., J. Thomson, and A. McMahon. 1996. *The Australian Welfare State: Key Documents and Themes.* Melbourne: Macmillan.

Wolf, J. 1989. The legacy of Mary Parker Follett. *The Bureaucrat*: 53-57.

Wolf, N. 1993. *Fire with Fire: The New Female Power and How It Will Change the 21st Century,* New York: Random House.

Wolfensberger, W. 1980. The definition of normalization: update, problems, disagreements and understandings. In *Normalization, Social Integration and Community Services,* ed. Flynn, R. J., and K. E. Nitsch. University Park Press.

——. 1983. Social role valorization: A proposed new term for the principle of normalization. *Mental Retardation* 21(6):234-239.

——. 1989. Human service policies: The rhetoric versus the reality. In *Disability and Dependency*, ed. L. Barton. London: Falmer Press.

——. 1991. A brief introduction to social role valorization as a high order concept for structuring human survices. syracuse, NY: Training Institute for Human Service Planning, Leadership and Change Aentry, Syracuse University.

Zola, I. 1975. In the name of health and illness. *Social Science and Medicine* 9:83–87.